Misused Words

No Mistakes Grammar Volume I

Giacomo Giammatteo

Copyright © 2016 Giacomo Giammatteo
All rights reserved.

Contents

The Words 1
Redundancies 111
Sayings 119

Final Note: 123
Other Books Coming Soon 124
Acknowledgments 127
About the Author 128

The Words

Misused Words
Misusing words when you speak gives an impression that you probably don't want to give.

Misusing words when you write is even worse, because it's permanent. Someone might forget what you said, but if it's written, well…it's there to refer to forever. With that thought in mind, let's try to get it straight.

Don't get me wrong. I'm not here to *tell* you how to write. I have a difficult enough time myself. When I send a manuscript to my editor, Annette, I get it back with more editing marks than you can imagine.

So what is my goal? To see if I can help even *one* person improve their writing or speech enough for them to be happy with it. If I sell a few books in the process, my animals will be happy. (All proceeds go to the animals on my sanctuary.)

I wrote this, and later I decided to split it into three books—one for the ordinary people, the ones who only want to see what they're doing wrong, one for people who rely on words for business communication (and who *need* to get it right), and one for the maniacs—like me—who simply want to get things right for the sake of being right.

Misused Words —which consists mostly of misused words and sayings (and a few redundancies)—the things you'd encounter in everyday life, covers almost 200 everyday misused words (187).

The other book—*Misused Words for Business*—covers the same points (not the same words) as the first, but also includes sections on Absolutes (words that shouldn't be modified) Business Redundancies, Capitalization, (a horrible misuse in business) Compound Modifiers, Mispronunciations, Punctuation, Sayings, and Times and Dates. It's not a complete grammar book, but it does cover a lot of territory.

The third book covers more redundancies, more absolutes, capitals, eponyms, flat adverbs, initialisms and acronyms, Latin phrases, a repeat of the mispronunciations (because it's needed), plurals of compound words, and more.

Let's face it, the last thing you want anywhere—but especially in business writing—is to have the meaning of your words taken the wrong way. So, whether you write cover letters, resumes, business proposals, or only emails to colleagues, get the book and learn to do it right.

It's a sin, but if you read enough blogs, and you know what you're looking for, you'll see hundreds—if not thousands—of mistakes every week. I have even caught grievous errors on grammar sites.

If you're going to write about grammar, you should make all efforts to get it right. I would never think of correcting someone's grammar in public, and yet one of the few TV shows I watch features a character who does just that. I wouldn't object, except he makes grammar mistakes—obvious ones.

My theory is that if you're going to have a character correct grammar, he better damn well be free of grammar mistakes.

Another note:
I thought about using definitions from dictionaries, but half of them I couldn't understand, so I tried to make my own definitions. I hope that worked out okay.

In some cases, quotes of famous people were used. I got these from Brainy Quote, which can be found here.
http://www.brainyquote.com

Throughout the book I used 🐗 as a symbol for a tip, or a way to remember how to tell the difference between words.

🐗 (Dennis) is my pet wild boar. We rescued him when he was only a few days old, and he's been with us for five years now. Of course, he's a little bigger, weighing in at about 400 lbs.

When we first got him, he was 12 lbs. In any case, I used an image of a wild boar to draw attention to a particular section/tip. I hope it will help you remember it.

Misused Words
In the 'old days' the written word was not only the preferred method of long-distance communicating, it was the *only* method. Marriages were arranged, business partnerships discussed, terms decided upon, and deals concluded. Heads of state negotiated treaties and settled territory disputes using 'words.'

Then came the telephone, and the airplane, and other forms of modern transportation and communication, and things changed. Emphasis shifted from the written word to the spoken word.

Transportation made getting together in person much easier, and less expensive, and if that wasn't possible the telephone sufficed as a backup. The result was that the written word faded into near obsolescence, and the generation that embraced this new technology couldn't have been happier; grammar had never been more than a necessary evil ~~anyways~~ anyway.

And then something strange happened. Technology advanced so rapidly that the planes and phones that had pushed writing and grammar into the background, and damn near buried them, were catalysts for bringing them back. Well at least one aspect of the technology.

According to Mashable, there were about 145 billion emails *per day* being sent as of November 2012. That's *billion* not million. No matter how you look at it, that's a lot of email.

Email single-handedly pushed writing back to the forefront of communication. Thanks to email, writing made a resurgence. The problem was it didn't bring grammar with it.

For some reason many people seem to think they don't have to 'write right' when using email. They view it like a trip to the corner store late at night, when it's okay to go wearing a T-shirt, or with your hair in curlers, or unshaven.

Corner store aside, it is not okay to send your emails, or any other communication, out that way. Don't do it—even if you're sending a message to friends or family; it will get you into a habit of being sloppy. And trust me, *you* might think it's okay. Your friends might think it's okay. Even your colleagues might say it's okay. *But it's not.* And it never will be.

Draft a sales proposal that has sloppy wording and your prospect will take notice. They'll wonder if that same sloppiness will show up in your company's products or customer service.

Hit the 'send' button on an email with your resume attached, and the person evaluating it *will* notice a mistake—trust me. I have spoken to a lot of human resource people who told me that mistakes were one of the first things they looked at. In fact, I published a book—*No Mistakes Resumes*—that deals with that subject.

I don't blame you. I understand how difficult grammar is, and even worse, how boring it is if you aren't interested in it. But it doesn't mean you shouldn't learn, or that you can't learn.

Don't worry; I'm here to help.

Vocabulary

Depending upon which study you read, the average person has a vocabulary of somewhere between 8,000 and 20,000 words. The writing vocabulary would be slightly less. Let's assume for a minute that we're talking the lower end of this—say 7,500 words. That's still a lot of words to remember, or, to mix up. But this list I'm providing you is much shorter. It's about 200 words (187), and these constitute the majority of the mixed up and misused words in ~~every day~~ *everyday* usage.

So without further ~~adieu~~ ado, we'll get started.

Words:

A/an:

A mistake I often see is the misuse of the indefinite articles 'a' and 'an.' The rules are simple, yet people often get them confused.

A—You use 'a' in front of a word beginning with a consonant *sound*, regardless of spelling. So, it would be: a fox, a dog, a university (the 'u' makes a 'y' sound), and yes, it would be *a* historic event. (Historic is pronounced with an 'h' sound.)

An—You use 'an' in front of words beginning with a vowel 'sound,' again, regardless of spelling. So, it would be an elephant, an ostrich, an antelope, and an honor. (In the word honor, the 'h' is not pronounced.) Words beginning with 'h' and 'u' seem to be the ones that confuse most people.

A lot/alot:

This is an easy one. *Alot* is *not* a word. It is *always a lot,* spelled as separate words.

A while/awhile:

This distinction is primarily a usage problem. When used as a noun phrase—*a while*—it typically follows a preposition.

Example: 'I think I'll stay **for** *a while*.'
When it is used as an adverb it takes the one-word format and follows verbs, *never a preposition*.

Example: 'If it's all right with you, I'll stay *awhile*.'

🐃 : If the word you're looking for follows a preposition, such as 'after, for, in…' use the two-word format, '*a while*.' If it follows a verb, use '*awhile*.'

Accede/exceed:

Accede—means to agree or approve of something. It can also mean to assume an office or title.
Note: *accede is usually followed by the word 'to.'*

Exceed—means to excel or be greater than. (On a resume you might see this under the accomplishments section—sales *exceeded* quota for region by 45%.)
🐃 : Try to think of 'exceed' as *excelling*. They both begin with 'ex.'

Accept/except: I have *accepted* the fact that everyone is incompetent—*except* me.
Accept=to receive a gift, to agree, accept an invitation, accept your responsibilities, accept a package…

I *accepted* responsibility for doing the project; no one else was doing it right.

Except=exclusion. (In most cases, you could substitute 'but' for *except*.)
All the soldiers, *except* one, died at the Alamo. I would go to Italy, *except* I have no money.

🐃 : Try to remember *accept* is associated with agree, like if your

spouse tells you it was your fault, and you wisely say, 'Okay, I *accept* that.' Agree and Accept both begin with A.
And *except* means exclusion. Both begin with 'Ex,' same as exceed.

Quote: 'We must *accept* finite disappointment, but never lose infinite hope.' ~ Martin Luther King, Jr.

Accidently/accidentally: This mix up is simply a spelling error. *Accidently* is *not* a word, it's simply how many people mispronounce—*accidentally*.

Accommodate: This is another spelling mix up. Many people spell it with one 'm.' The easy way to remember this is that both 'c' and 'm' are doubled.

Ad/add: An 'ad' is an advertisement and to 'add' is to increase in number, or find the sum of. Like adding a room to your house, or adding items to the grocery list.

🐎 : This one is simple to remember. The one with two 'd's' is the one meaning increase in number—you've *added* a 'd.'

Adapt/adept/adopt: I *adopted* a policy of flexibility long ago, and as a result, I am *adept* at *adapting* to almost any situation.

Adapt=to change things. To learn to live with changes in life. My grandfather, who was from Italy, had to learn to *adapt* to the new lifestyle he *adopted*.

Adept=an expert, a skilled person. The guy with the silk suit was an *adept* card player. He was *adept* at manipulating cards.

Adopt=to choose or take on as your own. The newlyweds couldn't have children so they *adopted* one. The baby was *adopted*.

🐃 : This is also an easy one. Look at the middle vowels in the three words: 'a, e, and o.'
Adapt has an 'a,' think of *adjust*.
Adept has an 'e,' think of *expert*.
Adopt has an 'o,' think of *orphan*.

Quote: 'Intelligence is the ability to adapt to change.' ~ Stephen Hawking

Adverse/averse: I am *averse to adverse* reactions.
Aside from the pharmaceutical company ads where they mention over and over and over again the *adverse* effects you might experience from taking their drugs, not a whole lot of people use these words. And that is why it is even more important that you get them right. If there's anything worse than using two-dollar words when they're not needed, it's using two-dollar words the wrong way.

Adverse is an adjective meaning unfavorable, like the above example of *adverse* reactions to drugs. Or perhaps you went hiking and a storm moved in, presenting you with *adverse* conditions, as in, the storm presented us with *adverse* conditions on Mt. Shasta.

Averse means opposed to/against. On a resume you might see someone say they are not *averse to* rolling up their sleeves, or not *averse* to doing hands-on work.

🐃 : Try to remember an *adverse* reaction to drugs, and that both drugs and *adverse* contain the letter 'd.'

🐘 And in almost every case, *averse* is followed by the word 'to.' I can't think of a case where *adverse* would be followed by 'to.' Also, think of *averse* as having a similar meaning as *against,* as in, I'm not *against* rolling up my sleeves.

Quote: 'I'm not *averse* to helping Wall Street when it helps Main Street.' ~ Ben Nelson

Advice/advise: I *advise* you to take my *advice*. (The headhunter *advised* Jane to take the job offer, but she ignored his *advice* and stayed where she was. She regretted it.)

Advice is a noun, and normally reflects someone's opinion or suggestion. Advice is something you *give (or take)*.

Advise is a verb, and represents the giving of *advice*. (You might find this in a resume listed as 'advised board on strategy for acquisition candidates.') Advise is something you *do*.

🐘 : You give or take *advice*, and you *advise* someone.

Quote: 'When your mother asks, 'Do you want a piece of advice?' it is a mere formality. It doesn't matter if you answer yes or no. You're going to get it anyway.' ~ Erma Bombeck
'I have found the best way to give *advice* to your children is to find out what they want and then *advise* them to do it.' Harry S. Truman

Affect/effect: These words are often confused because both of them function as nouns and verbs.
Affect as a verb means to have an influence on, or to stir or move.

1. The company layoffs *affected* the ~~moral~~ morale of the employees.
2. The president's speech on foreign policy *affected* the listeners, stirring emotions.
Affect is seldom used as a noun.

Effect as a noun means the result of something or the consequence of some action. (The *effect* of the layoff was a drop in morale.)
Effect as a verb means to bring about. The president's speech *effected* a change in policy.

🐘 : Although these words can both function as nouns/verbs, and both share the 'influence' meaning, there is a way to get it right *most* of the time.

Affect is almost always used in the verb form, so think of *action*, which also starts with an 'A.'
Effect is typically used in the noun form. Think of the 'end result.' (Even though 'end result' is redundant.)

Quote: 'To *affect* the quality of the day, that is the highest of arts.' ~ Henry David Thoreau

Aid/aide/ade: The politician, along with his *aide, aided* the sick and injured, by giving them *ade*.
Aid means to provide help or assistance.

Aide is an assistant or a helper, like 'the general's aide.'

Ade is a fruity drink, like a lemonade.

🐘 : Try to remember that the difference between *aid* and *aide* is that

11

the one with the 'E' is an employee, a person. The confusion comes because the past tense of *aid* is aided. Also remember that *ade* is just like lemon*ade*.

Afterward/afterwards

This rule applies to 'afterward, anyway, (despite what NYPD Blue says) backward, forward, onward, toward, untoward, and all the others.' It is 'afterward'—no 's.' Using the 's' is good in the UK, but the US preference is no 's.'

So, '*anyways,*' when you're writing, check it '*afterwards*' and take out the trailing 's' on each of the words.

All together/altogether:

Altogether is an adverb. It means entirely or completely.

The Wi-Fi service went out *altogether.* (Went out completely.)
All together is a phrase that means in a group.
Mrs. Johnson's fifth-grade class sang *all together.* Or Mrs. Johnson's fifth-grade class *all* sang *together.*

🐗 : If you can replace *altogether* with completely, or utterly without losing any meaning, then you are probably using the right word. And note that *all together* can be separated in the sentence and not lose its meaning, as in the example above.

Quote: 'If I play hard to get, soon the phone stops ringing *altogether.*'
~ Mason Cooley

Aloud/allowed: *First he thought it, and then he said it **aloud**, 'Smoking is not **allowed** on campus.'*
Aloud means to speak out loud.

Allowed has many meanings, but the majority of usage deals with permission or making provisions for.
We run an animal sanctuary, but we don't allow the animals in certain parts of our house.
*Monica's schedule was tight, but she **allowed** herself half an hour a day for reading.*

🐃 : The easiest way to remember this is that *aloud* contains the word *loud*.

Quote: 'A child who is *allowed* to be disrespectful to his parents will not have true respect for anyone.' ~ Billy Graham

Already/all ready: Are you *all ready*, because we're *already* late?
Already is an adverb. It means prior to, or previously, or so soon. It *almost always* implies time.
*Bob got to the meeting five minutes early, but his boss was **already** there.*

All ready is a phrase that means you are prepared.

🐃 : Remember that *all ready* consists of two words, and the phrase *all ready* refers to more than one person. You wouldn't say, I'm *all ready* to go. If it's just you, you'd say, I'm ready to go (or you should say that).

Quote: 'There cannot be a crisis next week. My schedule is *already* full.' ~ Henry A. Kissinger

Alright *or* all right: Some people still think that 'alright' is 'all right' but the majority of grammarians think that using 'alright' is similar to using 'ain't.'

Many others disagree, and *alright* is listed in most dictionaries as acceptable, but when consulting the AP Stylebook, its ~~advise~~ advice is, *never* use 'alright.' So even though it is becoming more accepted as a standard word, why bother? My suggestion is to use 'all right.'

🐘 : When you're thinking of which word to use, remember that 'alright' *ain't* 'all right.'

Quote: 'It is *all right* for the lion and the lamb to lie down together if they are both asleep, but if one of them begins to get active, it is dangerous.' ~ Crystal Eastman

Note: I have to say, when researching the quotes for this one, the majority of quotes were by people who used *alright* and not *all right*. (What a shame!)

Altar/alter:

Altar is a noun, meaning a table, structure, platform, etc… used for religious rites.
The groom got nervous and the bride was left at the *altar*.

Alter is a verb, meaning to change or make different. To modify in some way.
The tailor rushed to *alter* the groom's tuxedo.
You can *alter* the document by clicking the edit button.

🐘 : The second vowel in the words are 'e and a.' Remember that *altar* and aisle both have an 'a.'

Quote: 'Human beings can *alter* their lives by *altering* their attitudes of mind.' ~ William James

'I have sworn upon the *altar* of God, eternal hostility against every form of tyranny over the mind of man.' ~ Thomas Jefferson

Altercation: A quick note about the word *altercation*. I have seen many writers use it to mean a physical fight, when its definition is 'a heated or angry dispute; a noisy argument or controversy.' It has been misused so often that it is in danger of becoming standard, and I blame this on TV more than anything.

Example: My wife and I have had many *altercations*, but we've never laid a hand on one another.

Alternate/alternative:

Alternate can function as a verb, an adjective, or a noun.
A person suffering from bi-polar disease might *alternate* between highs and lows.
A chessboard has *alternate* black and white squares.
An understudy for a Broadway play might get their big break if they are the *alternate* and has to fill in for the star one night.

Alternative can function as a noun or an adjective. Definition—being one of a number of possible choices.
If you don't like buying books from Amazon, you have plenty of *alternatives*.

When diagnosed with cancer, my friend looked for *alternative* treatments.
If the freeway has an accident on it, try *alternative* routes. (Not *alternate* routes.)

🐘 : Try to think of *alternate* as a back and forth between two things, as in the examples above: 'highs and lows,' 'black and white,' and 'understudy and star.'
On the other hand, *alternative* deals usually with multiple options—all of Amazon's competitors, multiple choices for treatment, many options on which roads to take.
So the way to remember it is that *alternate* usually deals with two, and it is a shorter word than *alternative*, which usually deals with multiple options.

Quote: 'For every failure, there's an *alternative* course of action. You just have to find it. When you come to a roadblock, take a detour.' ~ Mary Kay Ash

Among/between: As he prepared to address the crowd, the politician leaned toward his aide, and said, '*Between* you and me, there is a spy *among* our group.'
Among means more than two.

Between—there can be only two.
Remember the movie *Highlander,* where the 'immortal' men had to fight until death. The tagline of the movie was 'there can be only one.' With the word *between*, there can be only two.
Between is used only for sentences involving two items, and among for sentences involving more than two.

🐘 : Remember the 't' in between stands for two.

Note: And yes, for any of you wondering, the correct form is *between you and me,* not between you and I.

Amoral/immoral: Some people live normal lives, but are still judged *immoral,* while others embrace religion to conceal their *amoral* philosophy.

Amoral means having no moral standards. An *amoral* person might be indifferent to the fact that his neighbor is a thief.

Immoral means not conforming to the norm. An *immoral* person might aspire to becoming a thief.

🐘 : An *amoral* person has not standards, and an *immoral* one has bad standards.

Quote: 'About morals, I know only that what is moral is what you feel good after and what is *immoral* is what you feel bad after.' - Ernest Hemingway

Anxious/eager: Some people use anxious and eager as if they were the same word, with similar meanings. It is becoming more acceptable in common usage (which is a damn shame) but there *are* differences, meaningful differences.
'Anxious' stems from the word anxiety. The Merriam-Webster dictionary defines anxiety as:

A: an abnormal and overwhelming sense of apprehension and of fear often marked by such physical symptoms as tension, tremor, sweating, palpitation, and increased pulse rate.

Dictionary.com defines *anxious* as: full of mental distress or uneasiness because of fear of danger or misfortune; greatly worried.

I am *anxious about* meeting my ~~fiancé~~ fiancée's father, but *eager to* meet her mother.

Dictionary.com defines *eager* as: keen or ardent in desire or feeling; impatiently longing.

🐃 : Notice that *eager* is usually coupled with 'to,' and *anxious* goes with 'about.'

So, you wouldn't tell the hiring manager that you are *anxious to* come for an interview. You might be *anxious about* interviewing, but tell them you are *eager to* come for an interview. It will mean more to them.

Quote: 'No one is more arrogant toward women, more aggressive or scornful, than the man who is *anxious* about his virility.' ~ Simone de Beauvoir

'When a man is willing and *eager* the gods join in.' ~ Aeschylus

Any time/anytime:

Anytime is an adverb.

Any time is used as two words can be an adverbial phrase or an adjective (any) modifying a noun (time).

Example:
I like restaurants that serve breakfast at *any time* of day.

Considering the state of the economy, it's doubtful I'll be finding a job *anytime* soon.

Any one/anyone:

Definition:
Anyone is a term meaning any person.

Any one as the two-word form means one specific person.

Example:
In this day and age, *anyone* might be a spy.

Any one of your friends might be a traitor.

Any way/Anyway/anyways:

If you used to watch the TV show, NYPD Blue, you probably thought *anyways* was a word. It isn't. The word is *anyway*—without the 's.'

Definition:
Suppose you're interrupted in the middle of telling a story. In that case, you might continue by starting with the phrase, *anyway*...as in, *anyway, as we were driving to Dallas...*

Any way means, in any manner, as in, 'Get it done *any way* you can,' the frustrated teacher told his students.

We were late for the movie, but we bought the tickets *anyway*.

Ascent/assent:

Ascent is to climb, go up, advance in status.

Example: Her *ascent* into high society was a foregone conclusion.

Assent: Agree to, concur.
The bride's father assented to the marriage.

Example: Obama gave his *assent* to put more troops in the Middle East. (You could also say 'Obama put more troops in the Middle East.')

Quote: 'Do not despise the bottom rungs in the *ascent* to greatness.' ~ Pulilius Syrius

🐗 : Remember that *ascent,* the word with the letter 'c,' means to climb.

Assume/presume:

Assume: Means to take for granted, or to take on a duty, or a persona.

Example:
He *assumed* they would finish the project on time. (Took for granted)

He *assumed the role as head of the family, when his father passed away. (Took on as a duty)*

In mythological tales, the gods often *assumed* human forms. (Took on)

Definition: *Presume (verb)*
To *assume* something is true.

Example:
He *presumed* the project was completed because everyone went home early.

A defendant is *presumed* innocent until proven guilty.

Note: Assume and presume are close in meaning, but *presume* comes with a stronger conviction.

Quote: 'I shall *assume* that your silence gives consent.' ~ Plato

🐦 : Remember that *presume* is the stronger of the two, and that if you *assume*, you might make an ass of yourself. The old saying is: If you *assume*, you make an ass of *u* and me.

Attendance/attendants:

Attendant:
The primary use of attendant is as a noun, meaning one who waits on another, or one who is present. The parking *attendants* were all females.

Attendance is also a noun, but doesn't refer to a person. An example would be; class *attendance* was at a record level.

🐃 : The best way to remember the difference is that *attendance* has the letter 'c' in it. Remember '**c**lass attendance.' Also, an *attendant* almost always deals with a person. Try to remember *female* parking *attendants*, and it might help.

Backward/backwards:

This is an easy one to remember. In the U.S., you always use *backward*, without the 's.' In the U.K., you use *backwards*. (It's like all the other 'ard' words—afterward, forward, inward, onward, toward, etc.)

Bad/badly:

Bad is almost always an adjective, but the confusion comes from people thinking it is sometimes used erroneously when combined with *feel*, as in, 'Ever since I got this cold, I've been feeling bad.'

Most everyone thinks that sentence should read, '…feeling badly.' The reason it is *bad* is because the word *feeling,* in that context, is a linking verb, which means the adjective—bad—is modifying the subject, not the verb. The same reasoning applies to 'I feel good.'

Band/banned: This is easy. *Band* is a group of people or animals or things functioning together, like a musical group. *Banned* means to be barred or prohibited.

🐃 : Remember that *banned* is similar to 'canned' and in most cases if you're *canned* from a job, you're *banned* from the premises.

🐻 : Also remember that if you enjoyed the performance, you would give the *band* a *hand.*

Bare/bear:

Bare Means without clothing, or naked. It can also refer to the *bare* walls, etc.

It can also mean to reveal, as in, the woman *bared* her soul to the psychiatrist.

Bear

There are far too many definitions to list, but I've listed a few of the more common ones.

As a verb, it means to stay firm, as in, he could not *bear* the financial burden. (He could not *stand* it, could not *weather the storm.*)

Or to bring forth, as in to *bear* a child. A tree *bears* fruit. (As in, she would eventually come to *bear* three children.)

As a noun, a *bear*, as in a black bear or a polar bear. (The *bear* was huge. It weighed 1,500 lbs.)

🐻 : This is a crude way to remember it, but it works. In the word, *bare*, the *a* comes before *e,* and it means naked. Think of your *ass* being *exposed.* ('A' before 'e.')

In the other *bear*, the *e* comes before the *a*. Think of a hungry *bear eating* your *ass*. ('E' before 'a.')

Teachers might not be able to use that tip for their students, but for the rest of us it works.

Beside/besides:

Beside: Alongside, next to, as in, she sat *beside* me on the bus. Or, I sat beside her at the speech/movies/theater, etc.

Besides: Means also, furthermore, in addition to, etc.

Example: We're going to the wedding because we accepted the invitation; *besides*, I'm the best man. Or, *besides* the towels, bring an umbrella.

Blond/blonde:

Definition: A golden, or yellowish-brown color. As an adjective, it is used to describe a person, as in the often seen and heard phrase—the blonde bombshell.

As a noun, it refers to a person who has such color hair, such as the sexist phrase, the dumb 'blonde.'

Since English doesn't use word-endings to distinguish the male/female attributes of a word—as in blond/blonde or brunet/brunette—the distinction between the versions soon got lost. Now, it is most accepted to use 'blonde' as a female noun, and 'blond' as its male counterpart; however, 'blond,' when used as an adjective, is often found used for both genders (especially in the U. S.), and no one seems to make a fuss about it. Example—he has *blond* hair, or he is a *blond*. On the contrary, it could be she has *blonde* hair, or she is a *blonde*. Some people refuse to give up the 'e' when using blonde as a female noun or adjective. For the time being, I don't think it matters.

🐘 : Remember the word with the 'e' refers to *her*. (Which also has an 'e.')

Board/bored:

Board:
A piece of lumber used for many purposes, such as building a house, deck, etc. Board can also refer to something used for display purposes, as in, the teacher wrote lessons on the (black)board.

Bored:
Bored can mean different things, that aren't closely related. In one sense, it means to drill a hole through, as in, the carpenter *bore* a hole through the 4x4 post.

It can also mean to become *disinterested*, as in, *we went to the movie, but it bored us.*

Furthermore, it can be used as the past tense of the verb *to bear,* as in, she *bore* three children.

🐘 : Try to remember that *board* contains the word *oar* and both are made from wood.

🐗 : *Bored* contains the word *ore*, and you *bore* through the ground to get *ore*.

Bore/boar/boor:

Bore: As a noun it means a person that is dull or tedious. As a verb it means to drill through.

Example:
Boar:
A wild boar. (My buddy, Dennis, is a wild boar. I use a wild boar image for tips.) (Also refers to adult males of several mammals.)

Example:
Boor: *A crass person, with no manners.*

🐗 : Remember that you drill through *ore* and that *ore* is contained in *bore* (which means to drill).

Borrow/lend/loan:

Borrow: Means to ask for something with the understanding that you will return it (or something of equal value), as in, let me *borrow* your car for the day. I'll bring it back tomorrow.

It can also mean to *borrow* or *use* something abstract, as in, I *borrowed* your idea for remodeling the kitchen.

Lend: Lend is the opposite of *borrow*. You borrow *from* and lend *to*. An example might be; I'm going to *lend* him five hundred dollars.

Or, I *lent* (past tense) him my car.

Loan: Loan should not be used as a verb. You don't *loan* someone money. You might provide a *loan,* but that's a different story. (And usually a bad idea.)

🐘 : Remember that *loan* is not a verb. You don't *loan* someone money, but if they *lend* it to you, or if you *borrow* it from them, that constitutes a *loan.*

🐘 : Also remember, that you *lend to* and *borrow from.* You can't *borrow to* a neighbor or *lend from* a friend.

Both and either are words that are overused—similar to had and that, but in a different perspective. It is especially true when the conjunctions 'and' and 'or' are present. One way to know if 'both' is needed is to remove it and see if the meaning of the sentence changes.

Example—*Jim both robbed and killed the foreigner.* Wouldn't it be the same if you said, *Jim robbed and killed the foreigner?* It would, so why use 'both?'

The same holds true for use of the word 'either.' Look at this sentence: The hostess was going to serve *either* shrimp or lobster. How does that differ from—the hostess was going to serve shrimp or lobster?

🐘 : Remember, remove the words from the sentence and see if the meaning changes. If it doesn't, leave them out.

Break/brake:

Break: Means to separate into pieces, as in, *I dropped the glass and broke (past tense) it.*

An escape plan, as in, *the prisoner made a break for it.*

Brake: Means to slow down or stop action, or, something that does this for you. Examples are—a *brake* pedal on a car, or, he used the *brake* to stop.

Breath/breathe:

You take a deep *breath*, but you *breathe* deeply. Or it's rapid *breath*, but you *breathe* slowly.

🐗 : Remember that *breath* is a noun, and *breathe* is a verb. There is no extra 'e' in breath, and there is no 'e' in noun. But there *is* an extra 'e' in breathe and there is an 'e' in verb.

Brunet/brunette—see blond/blonde

Can't/cannot:

Can't: Can't is a contraction for cannot, as in, I *can't* pick Joey up because I have a doctor's appointment. As you can see, it is easy to substitute *cannot* for *can't* and the meaning is the same.

There is one circumstance where *cannot* is awkward, and that is when you use a 'wh,' as in, *why can't I go to the movies?*

Try the substitution and see. *Why cannot I go to the movies?* It doesn't sound right. Or, what *can't* you do? What cannot you do? Or, where *can't* you go? Where cannot you go?

See what I mean? Aside from the 'wh' examples, the words are interchangeable.

🐘 : Remember that you shouldn't use *cannot* 'when' you have a 'wh.'

Capital/capitol:

Capital: A capital is a town/city that is the official seat of a government, as in, Austin is the *capital* of Texas, or Sacramento is the *capital* of California.

Capital might also mean the center of an industry, as in, Silicon Valley is the semiconductor *capital* of the world, or New York is the financial *capital* of the U.S.

It might also mean financial assets, as in, the start-up company went public to raise more *capital*.

Capital may also mean non-financial assets, as in, the republican candidate has the political *capital* to earn the nomination.

It might also mean extreme, as in, he was committed of a *capital* crime.

Capitol: Capitol is a building (or several buildings) where a state legislature meets or the building in Washington, D.C., where Congress meets.

🐗 : Remember that unless you're referring to a building, you want *capital*.

Example: He committed a *capital* offense in front of the *capitol*, and was convicted of *capital* murder.

Cent/scent/sent:

Cent: A cent (in the U.S. is a penny) but it is also 1/100 of a dollar. It represents that for the euro (€) also.

Scent:
A scent is an identifiable odor, as in, *I love the scent of honeysuckle in the spring*.

It can also mean the *scent* of an animal, as in, the skunk left a distinct scent while passing by.

It can also identify the ability or degree of smell, as in, the pigs *scent* was remarkable. It could find truffles three feet under the ground. (I can testify to the remarkable *scent* of pigs, as we have an animal sanctuary and I have seen them in action.)

Sent:
Sent is the past tense of 'send,' as in, my mother *sent* me to the store. Or, he *sent* me a package/email/text, etc.

President Obama *sent* more troops to Iraq.

🐘 : Remember that the one with the 'c' and no 's' is for currency. Of the other two, *sent* is more like *send*, and *sent* is the past tense of *send*.

Cite/sight/site:

Cite: Means to refer to an authority, or quote an authority. Lawyers are well-known for *citing* case law when they defend a case.

Police might also *cite* you for violating a law.

You might also be *cited* for bravery in the military.

Sight: Sight is the ability to see.

If something is 'out of sight' then you can't see it.

An aim, or a device used to aim, as in, the sniper *sighted* the target through his *sights*.

The foreseeable future, as in, the shipwrecked sailor lost *sight* of rescue as there was no land in *sight*.

Site: A *site* is the location where a building or structure has been or will be constructed, as in, the new office was built on the building's former *site*. Or, the construction *site* was littered with nails.

A common name for a URL, and short for *website*, as in, the reference material can be found on my *site* (website).

Examples: To 'cite' Sandra Day O'Connor became commonplace after her appointment to the supreme court.

The 'sight' of the tall ships in the harbor was amazing.

The 'site' for the new county morgue was approved by the city council.

🐂 : Remember that you need *light* (spelled like sight) to see, and *sight* is like see.

Complement/compliment:

Complement: There are two kinds of compliments, the flattery kind, and the *complement* that is associated with completion.

Flattery would be, she was *complimented* by everyone on the look of her new earrings.

Completion would be, her new earrings *complemented* her lovely blue eyes.

Example: She *complimented* him on how well the tie *complemented* his suit.

🐂 : Try to remember that the 'e' in *complement* stands for 'extra.' That's close enough to help you get it right. (Ketchup and mustard are *complements* for your food.)

Could not care less/Couldn't care less or Could care less.

You hear people say this both ways, but only one way is correct. The proper way is to say You *could not* (or couldn't) care less, not you *could* care less.

If you *could not* care less, it means you *could not* think any lower of someone, therefore, you despise them. If you *could* care less it could mean anything from you love them, to you hate them, but still not as much as you could. So, if you really want to say the worst to/about someone, say 'I *could not (or couldn't)* care less.'

Counsel/council:

Counsel: Advice or expert opinion, as in, legal *counsel.*

If you are charged with a crime, you might seek legal *counsel.*

Council: A group of (usually) respected people brought together to offer *counsel* or advice on problems and/or strategy.

Example: The lawyer gave *counsel* to the church *council.*

➤ : If you can 'give' counsel, then it's *counsel, not council.* You cannot give *council.* The priest *counseled* the parishioner. (He *gave counsel—* not *council.*)

Creak/creek:

Creak: To make a squeaking sound, as in, how floorboards *creak* when walked on.

Creek: A *creek* is a small stream (usually shallow) that often feeds a larger *creek* or river.

It can also mean a member of the Creek Indian tribe.

🐃 : Remember that both the stream/*creek* and the person *Creek*, contain the word 'reek' in the spelling. And they are the only ones who can technically 'reek.'

A 'creak'—or a sound—cannot emit an odor.

Cue/queue:

Cue: Most people think of a *cue* as a cue stick, a long (about 4') tapered piece of wood with a leather tip used to strike the cue ball in the game of pool or billiards.

Queue: A line (often long) of people or cars/vehicles. Think of the long lines at a popular movie or what you used to endure at the DMV.

A *queue* might also mean a series of commands waiting to be processed on a computer.

🐃 : Remember that a 'cue' is shorter than a 'line' and the word 'cue' is shorter than the word 'queue.'

🐃 : Or remember that the word 'cue' means a stick and that both cue and stick both have the letter 'c' in them.

Dates (B.C. (before Christ) is used *after* the date; A.D. (*anno domini,* 'in the year of the Lord') appears *before* the date. So you write Julius Caesar died in 44 B.C. And his nephew, Octavius Caesar, the Emperor Augustus, died in A.D. 14.

There has been a lot of debate lately about the use of BC (before Christ) and AD (anno domini) [in the year of our Lord]. People want to substitute them for CE (Common Era) and BCE (Before Common Era) but in their proposal, they keep the dates the same. So the year '1,' the year of our Lord, is still the divider, but instead of saying why—that Christ was born then—they refer to it as the 'common era.' A bit ridiculous, if you ask me. I'm for sticking with what we have.

Desert/dessert

Desert: A dry patch of earth that receives little rainfall and normally experiences extreme temperatures.

Most people think of *desert* as a hot, barren, sandy region, but there are *deserts* in Antarctica also. A *desert* is defined more by the amount of annual rainfall (less than 10 inches) than temperature.

Because of the lack of rainfall, *deserts* (hot or cold) have little vegetation.

Dessert: A *dessert* is a dish (usually sweet) served at the completion of a meal. It might be fruit, a sweet, pastry, or ice cream. Originally, this custom might have started as a means to clear the palate. Now it is thought of more as a 'treat.' Whenever I go out to eat, I usually opt for tiramisu as the *dessert*.

🐘 : Remember that a *dessert* is something you might want 2 of, and there are 2 s's in *dessert,* and only 1 's' in *desert*.

Device/devise

Device: A *device* is an object made to do one or more functions, as in, a glucose monitor is made to test the level of a person's blood sugar.

A *device* might also mean a writer's 'tool' used to advance a plot, or introduce new characters, etc.

Devise: To plan or come up with a new idea, as in, he *devised* a new medical *device*.

🐘 : Think of *devise* as coming up with a strategy, and both strategy and *devise* have the letter 's.'

Dragged/drug

Dragged: *Dragged* is the past tense of drag, and means to pull something (usually thought of as heavy), as in, he *dragged* the crate out of the way so the truck could park.

On a computer, you can also *drag* an icon to another position using a mouse or trackpad.

Drug: A *drug* is a pharmaceutical product used to treat or diagnose a disease. It can also be used in disease prevention.

A *drug* can also be an illegal product used for a person's pleasure, although it is normally referred to in the plural, as in, he's on *drugs*.

🐃 : A *drug* is a pharmaceutical.

Some people use 'drug' as the past tense of 'drag.' It seems to fit, so the usage seldom raises eyebrows, but if you research it, you'll see that 'dragged' is the preferred use.

So, you shouldn't say, 'I drug' him into the alley, but rather, 'I dragged him into the alley.' Although—unless there's a damn good reason—you shouldn't be *dragging* anyone into an alley.

Dual/duel

Dual: Having two parts, as in, some cars used for driver's education have *dual* brakes, or even *dual* steering wheels.

Duel: In the past, a *duel* was a formal combat between opposing parties, usually over a point of honor. Before the common use of handguns, the *duels* were fought with swords. Now a *duel* has come to mean any form of combat (though normally physical) between parties to decide the victor.

🐃 : Remember that the 'e' is for engage. To *engage* in a *duel*, both engage and *duel* have an 'e.'

Eg/ie/ergo/etc.

E.g.,: e.g., is a Latin abbreviation for exempli gratia, and it means, 'for example.' It should be written in italics, with periods and lower case letters, and is followed by a comma.

E.g., means 'for example' and should be used for that, not for clarifying what you mean to say. Leave that job to *i.e.,*. Remember that *e.g.,* and *example* both start with the letter 'e.'

Ie: *i.e.,* is a Latin abbreviation for 'that is' and is used to clarify the meaning of something. It is written similarly to *e.g.,* and is followed by a comma as well. It should precede a clarification.

Ergo: A Latin abbreviation for 'therefore' and as such, is frequently preceded by a semicolon. It can also be separated by a comma or an em dash, depending upon usage.

Etc: This is an abbreviation for et cetera, which means, 'and so forth.'

It should never be used in the same sentence as including or includes, and it should be preceded by a comma.

Some people might think that the use of ergo, et al, i.e., and e.g., are pretentious, but they are perfectly fine, and common practice, especially in the legal and insurance professions. One other thing, etc., is used only for *things*. Use *et al* when referring to *people*. (Et al means 'and others,' so it is appropriate.)

Elicit/illicit

Elicit: Means to extract an explanation, as in, the detective *elicited* a confession.

Illicit: Means something that is illegal, not allowed or acceptable. Against the law.

Example: The suspect committed an *illicit* act, but the detective *elicited* his confession.

🐟 : Remember that *illicit* and *illegal* both start with 'ill,' and *elicit* and *extract* both begin with 'e.'

Embarass/embarrass — another misspelling of a common word. Both the 'r' and the 's' are doubled, like both the 'c' and 'm' are doubled in accommodate.

It would be *embarrassing* to misspell either *accommodate* or *embarrass*.

🐟 : Remember that *accommodate, embarrass,* and *misspell* all have double consonants. It will help keep them straight.

Emigrate/immigrate (emigrant/immigrant)
Emigrate: To *emigrate* is to leave a country/place of residence—think of 'export.'

Immigrate: To *immigrate* is to come *into* a country—think of 'import.'

Example: My grandparents *emigrated* from Italy and *immigrated* to the US.

🐃 : You use 'from' with emigrate, so you 'emigrate' from somewhere, and you 'immigrate' *to* somewhere.

🐃 : Emigrate from/immigrate to. *emigrate=export. Immigrate=import.*

Every one/everyone:

It is almost identical to the examples cited in 'anyone' versus 'any one.'

Every day/everyday:

'Everyday' is an adjective usually describing a daily ritual, as in, *everyday* life is boring.

While 'every day' is used to mean each single day, as in, I drink coffee *every (each) day.*

🐃 : The easy way to remember it is if you can use 'each' day instead of 'every' day, you're speaking of the 'every day' that's two words. Try it with the example above: I drink coffee 'each' day. See, it makes sense—the sentence *and* the coffee drinking.

Fair/fare:

The difference between fair and fare is simple. 'Fair' is unbiased, on an even keel, not pro or con, as in, 'He is a *fair* person.' Or 'It was a *fair* fight.'

Whereas 'fare,' when used as a noun, typically refers to the price you pay to ride a taxi, or a bus, or train, or plane, or ship. It might also refer to you as the fare, as in, 'the cabbie took his *fare* to Central Park.'

As a verb, *fare* might mean 'to experience' as in, 'He fared well, considering his handicap.' Or 'she fared poorly.'

🐖 : I always try to remember that *pair* is spelled like *fair*, and if you have two people to buy for you'd *buy a pair to be fair.*

Yes, it's a stupid example, but it works for me.

Famous/infamous/notorious

Notorious: Widely and, usually, unfavorably known, as in 'he was a notorious gunfighter.'

Lately, the definition has evolved to mean more of a notoriety for something not so evil, as in, 'the company was notorious for its ruthless reputation.' (Perhaps that is a negative connotation, but not necessarily evil.) In other words, the person, or thing, being described does not *have* to be evil, or even thought of in a negative light.

Infamous: This one is as it sounds. It basically means being famous for something bad or evil, as in Charles Manson is *infamous* for the murders he committed, or Richard Nixon is, arguably, the most *infamous* president. The word has a negative connotation, and is never used in a positive light.

Famous: This is the typical. Michael Jordan is *famous* for his basketball achievements Or, Michael Jackson is *famous* for his vocal/singing achievements.

The differences: While Michael Jordan might be *famous* for his basketball achievements, he is *notorious* for his golf gambling. And while Michael Jackson might be *famous* for his singing, he is *infamous* for his alleged pedophilia.

Farther/further

Farther is for physical distance and *further* is for the metaphorical.

Example: She ran *farther* than I did.

Further thought on the matter will do no good.

🐖 : Try to remember that the 'far' in *farther* means distance. If you do that, you'll be right 99% of the time.

Fateful/fatal

This one is easy. *Fatal* refers to death, while *fateful* is the inevitable. So if it was a *fatal* accident, the person was killed. If it was a *fatal* heart attack, the person was killed. But a *fateful* event means that it was determined by 'fate,' or it was bound to happen.

🐘 : Remember that *fateful* contains the word *fate*.

Fewer/less

Traditionally, the rule has been to use 'less' for nouns listed as plural nouns and 'fewer' for others. Example, he ate *less* pizza than she did. Or, he ate *fewer* pieces of pizza. The difference being pizza is a plural noun, while pieces is not.

This is all wonderful, except that there are too many exceptions to the rule. And there are too many citations throughout the ages, for the 'rules' to carry much weight.

Fiancé/fiancée

Fiancé is used to describe a man who is engaged, and fiancée to describe a woman. This comes naturally from the origin of the words—which are French.

These words are seldom used properly. Only one word is normally used—fiancé—so it is only used right when it refers to the man. We've gotten so accustomed to it, that it has become acceptable usage for the majority of people.

Flammable/inflammable

This is a tough one. Both 'flammable' and 'inflammable' mean the same thing. I can't think of another word where the 'in' version (any word with 'in' as the prefix) means the same thing—think about it.

Sane/insane, ability/inability, capable/incapable, destructible/indestructible, vulnerable/invulnerable… The list goes on and on, but I think you get the point.

The question arises, why do words as important as flammable/inflammable have the same meaning?

So that no one mistakes the meaning.

Originally, 'inflammable' meant it could easily catch fire. People got confused by the 'in' prefix, so they made 'flammable' mean 'inflammable,' too. It's confusing but safe. Now, they both mean the product might easily catch fire.

Foreward/forward/foreword

First of all, 'foreward' is not a word. Now that that's out of the way, let's focus on the other two. 'Forward' (with an 'a') means 'direction,' as in, 'he was facing forward,' or 'move forward.'

'Foreword' (with the word 'word') means just what you might think. 'Fore'—meaning before—and 'word.' It is a section of a book that is 'before' the main work. It is usually written by someone else, typically someone who is respected.

🐗 : This is an easy one to remember. The 'word' in foreword relates to words.

Forth/fourth

Forth means 'forward' in time, as in 'go forth.' *Fourth* represents a number following third, as in 'he came in fourth' or 'he's the fourth one.'

It should be easy to remember. *Forth* starts with 'for' as in 'forward' and they both indicate movement. *Fourth*, starts with 'four' as in the number 'four.'

Foul/fowl

This should be one of the easiest mix-ups to remember. *Fowl* is only used when referring to birds, such as chickens, turkeys, pheasants, guinea hens, geese, etc. There are two types of *fowl*—land fowl and water *fowl*.

Foul refers to something wrong or nasty, as in a *foul* ball, or a *foul* odor.

The easiest way to remember this is to realize that 'fowl' contains the word 'owl'—a bird—and even though an owl isn't a *fowl*, it *is* a bird, so it should clue you in.

Good/well ???

I Feel Good

When I ask people 'How are you?', I typically receive a response of 'I'm well, thank you.' But is that the right response? Should you say good, or well?

This is a particularly sensitive issue, because in almost every interview situation candidates are asked something similar to 'How are you?' And you'll probably be asked that question by a number of people.

I know that most people don't want to say 'well.' I can tell by the change in cadence or the way they emphasize the word 'well.' But they feel it's proper grammar, so they respond with *well*. It's funny to watch the responses from people if you say, 'I'm good,' instead of 'I'm well.'

Some people raise their eyebrows and cast a sideways glance. Others hide a snicker, as if you've committed a grievous error.

But nobody questions you if you respond with 'I'm great.' Or 'fantastic.' The reason they don't is because those answers sound right. And they sound right because they are proper answers. The problem comes up because *well* is an adverb, but it's also an adjective.

I know what's going through your mind—the same thing that goes through everyone's mind…

But well is an adverb, and adverbs modify verbs.

As we all know, there are almost as many exceptions to rules as there are rules in the English language. I am going to try to put this explanation in the simplest form.

Which Is Correct—Good or Well?

When someone asks you, 'How are you?' or 'How are you feeling?' should I say good or well? Good is the preferred response to the question, 'How are you feeling?' (for clarity) but you can respond with either. It is also perfectly fine to respond with any adjective. So the following are all correct.

- I'm fine.
- I'm great.
- I'm good.
- Fantastic.
- I'm well.

Of the good or well controversy, 'I am well' is not wrong, but *not* for the reasons many people believe.

If you respond, 'I am well,' you are using well as a predicate adjective, not an adverb. A linking verb like am or are, or a 'sensing' verb like 'feel, taste, smell, and look' takes a predicate adjective not an adverb. So, for the same reasons that you say, 'that apple tastes good,' or 'he smells bad,' or 'she looks good,' (or great or terrible)…for those same reasons you say, 'I feel good.' Or 'I'm good.'

When you say 'I feel well,' and well is an adverb, you are literally saying that you 'feel' or 'touch' well. In other words your touch sensation is better than average. That is because 'feel' in that sense is an 'action' verb which requires an adverb.

Some people stand by a belief that while it might be all right to say good for some things, when it comes to health, well must be used. If you have a question about that, take a look at what Merriam-Webster has to say regarding the subject.

Usage Discussion of Good: An old notion that it is wrong to say 'I feel good' in reference to health still occasionally appears in print.

The origins of this notion are obscure, but they seem to combine someone's idea that good should be reserved to describe virtue and uncertainty about whether an adverb or an adjective should follow *feel*. Today nearly everyone agrees that both good and well can be predicate adjectives after *feel*. Both are used to express good health, but *good* may connote good spirits i*n addition* to good health.

One More Thing To Remember

If you have any questions about whether to use good or well, here's a rule for the future. Try to remember it.

When someone asks how you feel, and assuming you don't feel good, would you say, 'I feel bad,' or would you say, 'I feel badly.'?

I'm sure you would use 'bad.' And you would be correct. You might use 'terrible,' or 'horrible,' or 'sick,' or 'ill.'

And you would use those words because they are adjectives. You would only use *badly* if you were talking about the *action* of feeling, as in, he *feels badly* for a man whose fingertips were burnt.

When the 'Godfather of Soul,' James Brown, performed his legendary song—I Feel Good—he was using correct grammar, whether he cared or not. So the next time someone asks you 'How are you?' or 'How are you feeling?' take a deep breath, puff up your chest and shout it out, just like James Brown did so many years ago.

I Feel Good!

Or great, fantastic, wonderful, or any other adjective you want to use.

You can even use well, but if you do, say it with pride, knowing you're using an adjective, not an adverb.

For further reference, you can also check the AP Style Guide and/or the Chicago Manual of Style, Grammar Girl, Purdue's Online Writing Lab, or, Merriam-Webster.

Grateful/thankful

Grateful and thankful:
Example: At first blush, there doesn't seem to be much difference between these two words, but if you dig deeper, you'll see that 'grateful' is more of a 'state of being,' as in, you can be grateful you are a good person, whereas 'thankful' is more in response to something given. You can be 'thankful' for a gift, or even someone's love, but you're 'grateful' for being the person you are.

With that said, there is enough disagreement, or lack of agreement, on the subject to make it more than hazy. I don't think anyone will confuse your meaning no matter which word you use, and you can be *grateful* or *thankful* for that.

Gray/grey

These are the same words, simply variations in the spelling, and it's easy to remember. The 'a' stands for 'America' and the 'e' stands for 'England.'

Grisly/grizzly

These words should be easy to distinguish. Grisly means horrible, ghastly, gruesome, terrible, while 'grizzly' is usually referred to as an adjective for brown bear. Grizzly also means 'gray' or grayish hair, though it is seldom used that way.

The easiest way I found to remember it is grizzly and zebra both contain the letter 'z' and both are animals.

Guarantee/guaranty

There's a difference here, but one of the words is seldom used, except in the legal and insurance professions.

Guarantee functions as both a verb and a noun, and is used widely. 'I *guarantee* this will be done.' 'I offered him a *guarantee* on the car.'

Guaranty functions as a noun, and is almost exclusively used in the legal or insurance professions to represent something that is offered as a *guarantee*.

🐾 : To remember this, think of the letter 'y,' and ask yourself 'why' you should use this word.

Hail/hale

Hail, as a noun, is ice that falls from the sky, as in, it almost always hails preceding a tornado. It can also be used as a verb, as in, 'hail, Caesar.' You might also 'hail' a cab, or ask someone where they 'hail' from.

Hale means 'healthy,' as in 'hale and hearty' and other such expressions. There is also an old, out-of-date use as a verb, meaning to 'hale' or to 'haul' something, though I have never heard it used that way.

An easy way to remember it is that 'hail' has 'ail' in it—the opposite of hale—and if you 'ail' you're probably *not* hale.

Hanged/hung

Hanged is the past tense of 'hang' and is used when writing, or talking, about a person that was hanged.

Hung is the past participle of 'hang' and is used when writing, or talking, about an inanimate object that was 'hung.' You can't say, 'he was hung for his crimes.' It should be—he was *hanged* for his crimes.

🐃 : So, the sheets were 'hung' on the line to dry, but the man was 'hanged' for his crimes.

Hangar/hanger

A hangar is where you store or maintain an airplane. A hanger is what you hang your clothes on.

🐃 : It's easy to remember. The 'a' in hangar stands for *airplane*.

Heroin/heroine

Heroin is a highly addictive narcotic that is a derivative of morphine. Possession of heroin (one ounce or more) or sale of heroin, is a criminal offense punishable by a prison term.

A heroine is a female character (usually the lead) in a play or movie that possesses admirable courage or bravery.

As you can see, 'heroin' is a vile drug, while 'heroine' is a respected female hero. Not to say that a *heroine* couldn't use *heroin*, but she'd have a steep hill to climb if she wanted to continue being a *heroine*. The *heroine* of the play was arrested for using *heroin*.

Here's

Is it 'here's' or 'here are?' *Here's* has crept up on my 'grammar' list as the number two 'mistake' of all time, superseded only by 'there's.' The way the language is changing, I'm sure it won't be categorized as a 'mistake' for much longer. But for the time being let's look at why I list it as a 'mistake.'

'*Here's* ten things to put on your list.'

Why is this wrong?

Because it should be 'here are' ten things to put on your list.

Here's is a contraction for *here is*. It is no different than the number one error I see/hear, and that is 'there's.'

I think the best way to explain this is to show an article I wrote about the use of 'there's' on résumés, so here goes.

There's a Lot of Reasons...
...why I'm writing this post, and the heading of this sentence is one of the primary ones. To a growing number of people, the phrase, 'There's a lot of reasons,' and others like it are okay. They're acceptable. But to other people, in particular, resume screeners and gatekeepers...let's just say it will make them cringe.

What's Rong Wit Dat?
The correct way to write that phrase would be, 'There *are* a lot of reasons...' We use *are* because *reasons* is plural. You wouldn't say, 'We *is* going to the store,' or 'I *has* a reason for doing that.'

The misuse of *there's* has grown to be one of the worst mistakes in language these days, followed closely by the misuse of *here's*, as in 'Here's the reports you asked for.' And even, *where's,* as in 'Where's the reports I asked for?'

In all of the above cases the plural form should have been used. 'Here *are* the reports you asked for.' And 'Where *are* the reports I asked for?'

Many of the problems stem from the use of 'a lot.' It can be singular or plural. Look at these examples:
There is (there's) a lot to do.
There are plenty of places to park.

🐎 : One trick is to substitute *much* or *many* in place of *a lot.* If *much* fits, use *there's.* If *many* fits, use *there are.* In the sentences above, that would look like this: There's much to do. (You certainly wouldn't say there are *many* to do, would you?)
Or, *there are many* parking spaces. (Same thing—you wouldn't say, there are *much* parking spaces.)

🐎 : So, if the sentence contains *a lot* and you can substitute *much*, then use *there's, or there is*. But, if you can substitute *many*, then use *there are*.

I even saw this mistake on a big site in a post that was talking about—are you ready for this—grammar mistakes.

In case you're wondering, 'what's it gonna' hurt?' Let me give you a little insight from someone on the other side of the desk. I'm a headhunter. I know. A not-so-noble profession by many standards. But some of us take our work seriously. If a client gives me an assignment, and that assignment calls for a candidate with 'excellent communication skills,' I take that requirement seriously as well.

So? You Might Ask

So when I see a cover letter that starts out with 'There's a lot of reasons why I fit this job…' There are two thoughts that cross my mind, and only two:

- The candidate doesn't *know* they made a mistake using *there's* instead of *there are*.
- The candidate doesn't *care* they made a mistake.

The problem is that no matter which of those thoughts is correct, it doesn't bode well for the candidate. If I think they don't *know* the proper way to say it, I'm forced to wonder why I'd hire them. And if I think they don't care, I *definitely* won't hire them.

Bottom Line

This advice is not restricted to cover letters or resumes. Anything you write is subject to scrutiny and judgment, even your emails. And let's face it, you never know who will see them.

I'm sure that the majority of you have heard the old maxim, 'Anything worth doing, is worth doing right.' And I'm sure you take that to heart in your job. But try to remember, that rule applies to language as well.

Hear/here

Here is used as an adverb and indicates location. Here is the pen. Come here. Here is the dinner you ordered.

Hear is primarily used as a verb, meaning to listen. Or indicating the act of listening. She heard the music. *Hear* me out. Did you *hear* the sound of the squirrel?

🐘 : This is also an easy one to remember. The word that contains 'ear' is the one that deals with listening.

Hoard/horde

Hoard is used as both a verb and a noun. As a verb it might mean the act of hiding a treasure for future purposes, as in, the knight *hoarded* the treasure he found in the church. As a noun, it could mean the treasure itself. As in the 'dragon's hoard.'

A *horde* is a large or massive group, as in a 'horde' of gnats or a 'horde' of Mongols.

The way I remember it is a 'hoard' is spelled like 'board' and a *hoard* might be hidden under a *board*.

Home/hone (homed in or honed in)

I don't know of anyone who gets confused over home and hone, but 'home in' and 'hone in' are different. That comparison seems to be ripe for confusion, so let's try to set the record straight.

Home is a base of operations, or a *haven*. Home base, a home to live in, a place to call home, etc.

To hone is to sharpen something, as in, he honed the edge of the sword.

A missile 'homes in on' its target, in other words, it is guided to the target. And yet, I constantly hear people say 'hone in on.' That misused variation is gaining wider acceptance but it is obviously, and painfully, erroneous.

Perhaps no one will question your use of 'hone in on,' but if you use 'home in on,' you can substantiate it and be safe in knowing you're using it correctly.

🐗 : Think of a missile *homing in on* a target. (Aiming for a house.)

Hunger pangs or hunger pains

Hunger Pangs — these are traditionally referred to as hunger pangs, but they have come to be known as 'hunger pains.' It's a good thing, as most people seem to refer to them as hunger pains anyway. If you say, 'hunger pangs' someone will invariably give you a look, as if to say, 'what the hell are you talking about?'

However, if you wish to use the phrase correctly, refer those people to the Internet (or preferably here) to verify the usage.

Imply/infer

This is easy to decipher. To *imply* is to suggest or hint at something. To *infer* is to guess or deduce what the *implier* means. Remember that the person speaking is always the one who *implies* and the listener is the one who *infers*.

In/into (in means 'within' something.)

Example: The bottled water is *in* the refrigerator. But she walked *into* the house.

🐎 : A basic rule is that 'into' is an 'action' item, while 'in' implies 'within.' This isn't always the case, but most of the time it is. If you follow this guideline, you'll be correct most of the time.

Incidence/incidents

Both words sound alike. The mass noun, incidence—which is a plural noun—means the occurrence of something, as in, the *incidence* of malaria in Panama has decreased.

Incidents is the plural form of *incident* and means multiple *incidents,* as in, there were five *incidents* at the mall today.

Incredible/incredulous

These two words are similar, yet they're not. *Incredible* means difficult to believe even though it's true. It is *not* meant to be used as an intensifier, as in, that was an incredible apple; however, a 14-inch downpour that appears from nowhere *can* be *incredible*—difficult to believe, yet it *did* happen.

Incredulous is different, it is something that is difficult to believe because it is a lie, or wrong. If someone tells you he *accidentally* got caught with cocaine, he might be considered *incredulous*.

Inter/intra

Inter means 'between.' (Think of interstate. The freeways go *between* states.)

Intra means within, as in, an 'intrastate' highway. (It stays within the state.)

🐃 : Within a company, you might have *interdepartmental* struggles, like between engineering and operations. But if you had an *intradepartmental* memo, it might be for the marketing group only.

Irregardless

The definition of *irregardless*, is *regardless.* Both mean the same thing, although *irregardless* is considered 'nonstandard' by just about everybody.

Regardless means 'without regard' and by definition, 'irregardless' means 'without without regard.' Yes, it doesn't make sense.

So, *regardless* of what you think, using *irregardless* is wrong.

🐃 : My suggestion is to *not* use *irregardless,* but if you do, know that is not accepted English.

Isle/aisle

An *isle* is an island. Some people only use it to mean a 'small' island, but I've seen it used for descriptions of much larger ones.

An *aisle* is a passageway, as in, the bride walked down the 'aisle.' Or the 'aisle' of a grocery store, where the stocker might say the tomato paste is on 'aisle four,' when asked.

🐃 : This is easy to remember, as *isle* starts out just like *island.*

Its/it's

Seldom do three letters stir such confusion. And yet, *it's* easy to spot the differences.

It's (with apostrophe) is always, and only, a contraction—either for 'it is' or 'it has,' as in 'it's been raining.' (It *has* been raining.) Or 'it's' mine. (It *is* mine.)

Its (no apostrophe) is used for all other instances. So, you'd say, 'the company had *its* annual picnic on Saturday.' Or, 'the zoo displayed *its* panda bears last week.'

Even though *its* shows possession, *it's* (it is) like 'hers or ours or theirs,' it doesn't take an apostrophe.

🐃 : Remember *it's* is either it is or it has—nothing else.

Jam/jamb

Jam is a preserve made from sugared fruit, and 'jamb' is the side of a door or window, as in the *door jamb* or *the window jamb*.

🐃 : Remember you can *b*u*mp* into a door jam**b**, and both have 'b's' in the word.

Ladder/latter

Ladder is a device used to ascend or descend. It usually has wooden or metal construction (sometimes rope) and has a series of 'rungs' spaced between.

Latter means the last choice offered, as in the former or the *latter*.

🐃 : I try to remember it by the letter 'd.' *Descend* begins with 'd' and matches the 'd' in *ladder*.

Lie/lay/lain versus Lay/laid/laid

Perhaps one of the more confusing comparisons in the English language, *lie* and *lay* has long been disputed, and has even longer been misused. How often do you hear anyone use it in the proper sense, of 'yesterday, I *lay* down for a nap?' Probably close to never, unless you hang out with a band of nerdy grammarians. Usually, you'll hear, 'yesterday, I *laid* down for a nap,' and no one will bat an eye at that statement.

The correct way to say it is, 'I am going to *lie* down for a nap,' or 'I *lay* down for a nap, yesterday,' or 'There have been days when I *have lain* down for two naps.'

Write me a letter if you ever hear someone use it that way, though, as it might be a first.

On the other hand, *lay*, (when used as placed) is typically used properly. 'I am going to *lay* the pencil on your desk.' Or, 'I *laid* the pen there an hour ago.' Or, 'Yesterday, I *had laid* the eraser alongside the pen.'

Remember this: you shouldn't use *laid* if it is in conjunction with sleep, or rest—unless—it takes an object. So the statement, 'yesterday, I *laid* him down to sleep,' is correct, but 'yesterday, I *laid* down to sleep,' is not correct.

🐦 : If you can substitute the word 'place' for it, it is usually *lay* (present tense) or, if you can substitute placed, it requires *laid* (past tense). Examples: 'Place' [*lay*] the pencil on the desk. I 'placed' [*laid*] the pencil on the desk.

Not only does it tell you if it works or not, but indicates the tense (place=lay and placed=laid). But you couldn't say 'I am going to 'place' down to sleep.' Or 'last night I 'placed' down to sleep.' It sounds ridiculous and doesn't make sense.

Leach/leech

🐦 : Leech and 'eel' (The first three letters of 'leech' spelled backward) are both found in the water.

Lead/led

When I did research for my No Mistakes Resumes book, the mistake I saw most often was the misuse of *lead* and *led*. I did a search of my database, which contains almost twelve thousand resumes. From the search results I pulled up all the resumes that used the word 'lead.' I randomly went through the first three hundred, and in an astonishing *27%*, the person had used the present tense *lead* instead of the past tense *led*.

Here is an example from a resume:

- Developed prototype for new product geared toward revolutionized testing for…
- *Lead* efforts of twenty-seven engineers and brought in product on schedule and under budget.

As you can see, the first accomplishment was fine, done properly in the past tense using the word *developed*. The second, however, uses *lead* in the present tense, instead of *led*, which is the past tense of the verb.

This leads (present tense) me to believe that people don't have a good command of the English language. I was led (past tense) to this belief by seeing so *damn* many resumes with this same error.

This is one of the most common mistakes on resumes, but there are plenty of others. A few are listed below:

- Spelling errors
- Misuse of words
- Mixing up tenses

- Incorrect use of compound adjectives/modifiers
- Incorrect punctuation, including the dreaded semicolon

Don't worry. We will get to them all in time. Have ~~patients~~ patience.

Lessen/lesson

A 'lesson' is something taught or learned, as in, the student learned more of a 'lesson' than the teacher intended.

'Lessen' means to make fewer or decrease or reduce. *If you lessen the archers, you might lose the battle.*

🐃 : Lessen and fewer both have two occurrences of the letter 'e.'

🐃 : This 'lesson' is probably more for the adult crowd, as I'd hope the students know their *lessons* on *lesson versus lessen.*

Libel/liable/slander

Libel is the defamation of a person's name 'in writing,' or any form other than spoken words. Example: If you say something about a person 'in writing,' including on the Internet, then you are *liable* to be sued.

Slander is the defamation of a person's name 'not in writing.' So imagine you're a guest on a radio or TV talk show and you say something 'unflattering' about someone you might be *liable* for slander.

Slander has another legal requirement. The injured party must prove that they suffered a loss of income/money as a result of your *slander*.

In other words, a rap star, or anyone else, can't have you say something bad about them, see record sales soar, then sue for *slander*.

Liable means to be held accountable for, likely or susceptible to happen, as in, the obese man was *liable* to have a heart attack. Or, as a result of the tell-all book she wrote, she was *liable* to be sued. Or, don't step on the grass, or he's *liable* to get angry.

🐃 : A way to remember the differences is that the 's' in *slander* is for *speaking,* and the 'a' in *liable* is for *apt,* as in he's 'apt' to get angry, or he's 'apt' to have a stroke.

Lightening/lightning

I see this frequently, even among writer friends. 'Lightning' (without the 'e') is what occurs naturally in nature, an electrical discharge. 'Lightening' (with the 'e') means to lighten up, 'the marketing department wanted a *lightening* of the ad background.'

🐃 : The word *lightning* doesn't need the 'e' (energy); it has enough.

Literally

A lot of people use *literally* wrong. It's original meaning was accurate in the strictest sense, as in he took her words *literally,* and jumped off the bridge.

Today, the usage has changed. Many people use it, but *not* in the strict sense, as in, 'she literally died when she saw him dressed like that.' She might have been aghast, mortified, or appalled, but I doubt she died.

Loath/loathe

Loath means unwilling or reluctant. It is an adjective, and is almost always followed by 'to,' as in, 'she was 'loath to' admit her mistake,' or 'he was 'loath to' accept the stolen money.'

Loathe is a verb meaning to detest or abhor, feel utter disgust for, as in, 'she *loathed* the manner in which he conducted himself at the dinner table.' Or, 'he *loathed* gangsters and street thugs, but he had good reason; his father had been killed by a thug.'

🐃 : *Loathe* has an 'e' and the word 'verb' has an 'e.'

Loose/lose

This is an easy one to remember, and yet, many people confuse it. I have even seen many writers confuse it, which makes you wonder what kind of editor they have.

Loose means 'loose fitting,' unbound, unattached, while 'lose' is a verb which means you misplaced something, or 'lost' something or someone in another manner. An example might be 'the panicked mother 'lost' her child at the beach.' Or he 'lost' his keys. But the young man's 'loose-fitting clothes showed too much of his backside,' or, 'the knot was tied too loosely, and she escaped.'

🐃 : An easy way to remember it is to think of the extra 'o' as being 'loose,' or slack in a rope as in 'the noose was loose,' or a runaway moose, as in 'the moose was loose.'

Mantel/mantle

A *mantle* is a *coat* or a *cloak*. I haven't seen it used much of late, but the spelling and a few lingering sayings, continue to confuse people.

A *mantel* is the shelf above a fireplace (where you might hang stockings for Santa).

🐎 : There aren't many good ways to remember this one, but try to remember that a *mantel* is a *shelf*, and both contain the letters 'el,' in that order.

Marshal/martial

Marshal is the name of many occupations, but they all deal with law enforcement of some kind. It wasn't always this way. Hundreds of years ago, a *marshal* was a person who took care of the horses (in old Germany). Later, the word was associated with the leader of cavalry, and still later, a military officer similar in rank to a general. Napoleone Buonaparte had some of the finest *marshal*s ever. (And, yes, that *is* how to spell Napoleone's name. He was born in Corsica as Napoleone di Buonaparte.)

Now we have U.S. *marshals*, fire *marshals*, air *marshals*, etc. Notice the spelling is with a single 'l.' This is a word often misspelled with a double 'l.'

Martial means inclined toward war, but it is almost always used as an adjective for *martial arts*.

🐎 : Try to think of the 't' in *martial* as representing *tai chi*. If you can do that, you'll get this straight.

Meat/meet/mete

There aren't many triple homonyms in the English language, but they all seem to present problems and meat/meet/mete is one of them.

Meat is normally referred to as the flesh of an animal, like a steak or chicken. It can also mean the main/edible part of fruit or a nut.

Meet is to greet or be introduced to, as in, *it's nice to meet you.* It can also mean to wait for someone to show up, as in, I'll *meet* you at the bus stop, or I'll *meet* you for lunch.

Mete is to distribute (usually evenly) or to 'dish out' justice, as in, he *meted* out the punishment to the man who stole the horse.

🐎 : Remember that 'meat' contains the word 'eat' and you *eat meat.*

Minute (minit) and minute (mynoot)

Minute and *minute* are spelled exactly alike, but mean different things. These are called *homographs*. The language is full of them. Words such as wind/wind, read/read, lead/lead, etc. Examples—*Read (reed)* the book. He *read* (red) the book. Listen to the *wind* howl. *Wind* the clock. *Lead* the horse to the stable. Superman can't see through *lead.*

A *minute (pronounced minit)* is a measurement of time—1/60th of an hour. Example—give me a *minute,* and I'll be ready.

Something *minute* (pronounced my noot) is tiny, small. Example—the watch consisted of many *minute* parts.

🐘 : Try to think of the phonetic spelling of (mynoot). It has a 'y' and 'tiny' has a 'y.'

Moral/morale

Moral and *morale* look similar, but the pronunciation is emphasized on different syllables. *Moral* rhymes with plural and *morale* rhymes with corral.

Moral—as a noun—is used to indicate a lesson learned from an example or story, as in, Aesop's Fables, where each story had a *moral*.

As a plural adjective, it means virtuous, as in, his *morals* left a lot to be desired.

Morale, on the other hand, is a noun meant to indicate a person or group of people's spirits, as in, the human resource department felt *morale* was low after the board announced the merger.

🐘 : Since *morale* is associated with a person's *emotional* state, remember the word with the 'e' means emotional.

Must of/must have & should of/should have

I hear this far more often than I should, and it's not always from *uneducated* people. The bottom line is this—*must of and should of* are simply the result of people *mishearing* the common contractions for *must have* (must've) and *should have* (should've).

🐘 : Remember, there is no 'of' in must've or should've.

Novel (only used for fiction)

Novel might refer to a work of fiction, or to a new thought, as in, that's a *novel* idea.

It is not used to refer to a book that is nonfiction.

How to Use Numerals/Numbers When Writing

When writing, I like to spell the numerals 'one through ten' and use the actual numerals for those over ten. An example might be, *the farmer had six cows*. But you might write, *the farmer had 34 chickens*.

Since we're speaking about business writing and/or resumes, I thought I'd use a post I wrote about numbers as an example.

Everything You Need to Know About Numbers on Résumés

Numbers On Résumés
Before we get started, I'm going to briefly discuss numbers and numerals. By definition, a numeral is:

A word, letter, symbol, or figure, etc. expressing a number.

There are rules regarding when to use the word *numeral* versus *number*. I'm going to ignore those rules and use number/s for everything. Now back to looking at numbers.

Reading Résumés...
...is a boring job, the kind of job that can put you to sleep if you're not careful. That's why it's so important that the person writing the

résumé does everything in their power to keep the résumé screener awake and to make sure the screener doesn't get frustrated.

One of the worst offenders on résumés is inconsistency, and when we talk inconsistency— numbers (and everything dealing with them), take home the prize.

Rules

The rules governing writing numbers can be long and complicated. But even worse than that, the rules are often in conflict. The few that seem to be fairly consistent are the following:

- Spell out numbers from one to nine.
- Hyphenate compound numbers from twenty-one to ninety-nine.
- Don't start a sentence with a number.
- Use commas for numbers with more than three digits. (4,377 not 4377)
- If you use fractions, hyphenate them. (Two-thirds, not two thirds)

But like all rules, even these rules have exceptions. Which brings us to the point of this post—consistency. If you follow the few rules above, and if you're consistent with the use of numbers on a resume, you'll be way ahead of the game. So let's start with the first area of interest…

Dates

Résumés are full of dates: the year you graduated; the date range of each company; the date range of the positions you held; dates of accomplishments; dates of awards, etc. And quite often, those dates are expressed in as many different ways as there are dates.

There are many ways that would be acceptable. The important thing is to be consistent.

Months Spelled Out? Or Numbers?

The place where dates are used most are in the Work History section, and the biggest problems I see are that some people use numbers to represent months and some spell the months out. Either way is right, as long as you are consistent.

So, August 1999–May 2003 is perfectly fine, but so is 08/1999–05/2003, or even 8/99–5/03. The problems come up when someone starts out with one style and switches to another—usually to save space or to make it fit on one line.

I strongly suggest picking one style and sticking with it. My personal preference is using numbers combined with the full year, like this: 08/1999–05/2003.

On a side note, the punctuation separating the dates should be an 'en' dash, not a hyphen or an 'em' dash, and it should be used with no spaces surrounding it.

✗ 08/1999-05/2003 (do not use a hyphen)

✗ 08/1999—05/2003 (do not use an em dash)

✗ 08/1999 – 05/2003 (do not use spaces to surround punctuation)

✓ 08/1999–05/2003 (use an en dash, with no spaces)

Alignment
I suggest right-aligning the date range for each company. If you don't know how to do that, take a look at this video. And I suggest offsetting the dates for each position one or two tab stops left of the others.

Percentages
The most powerful parts of a résumé are often represented by percentages. Showing how much money you saved, or how many new accounts you brought in, or how much you improved yields, etc., can be very persuasive. And using percentages can be even more powerful when combined with dollars.

Example: Increased sales by $6 million, a 24% increase from previous year.

I used *6* instead of *six* to stay consistent within the sentence. It might not even be correct, but in my opinion it looks better and it has more impact.

Regardless of any rules cited above, I recommend consistency within a sentence whenever possible.

✘ Cut costs by $1.5 million on a seven million dollar budget.

✓ Cut costs by $1.5 million on a $7 million budget.

Bottom Line
A résumé is a simple document with a lot of complexity. One of the most important things you can do to improve your résumé is to eliminate mistakes. The other is to make it consistent. If you follow

the advice in this post, and take a close look at all the numbers you use, you'll be ahead of the crowd.

Onto vs. On to

You wouldn't say, the dog got 'on to' the sofa, but you would say the dog got 'onto' the sofa.
Onto is a preposition that means 'on top of' and that makes a clever way to straighten out the two. If you can use the word 'up,' you probably need 'onto,' as in, 'the dog got 'up on' the sofa.' Since you could use 'up' and still have it make sense, use 'onto.'

But if two kids were talking after English class and one said 'Let's move 'on to' the next class,' it wouldn't work to substitute 'up.' Try it.

'Let's move 'up to' the next class doesn't sound right.'

The other thing to remember is if the verbs 'hold' or 'move' are being used, there is a good chance it is 'on to' and not 'onto,' as in, 'he moved on to the next choice,' or 'she held on to the pen.'

✎ : Think of the old soul song from the 1960s, 'Hold On' by the Radiants.

Overdo/overdue

To *overdo* something is to overindulge, as in, eating or drinking too much. It is a verb. Example—don't *overdo* the drinking.

By contrast, *overdue* is an adjective and means something is *late* or *past due to be paid*. Example—the electric bill was *overdue*.

🐃 : It's easy enough to remember the difference. *Overdo* ends with 'do,' which is a verb, as is *overdo*.

And *overdue* ends with 'due,' as in the bill was *due*.

Palate/palette/pallet

A *pallet* typically holds 40 bags of Portland cement.

The painter's *palette* consisted of 96 colors.

Her *palate* was extremely sensitive, which allowed her to distinguish subtle tastes.

These three words constitute another triple homophone—all three sound the same, but are spelled differently and have different definitions.

Passed vs. Past

This should be another easy one, but it doesn't seem to be. People confuse it frequently. *Passed* is the past tense of *pass*, and should never be used in the sense of 'time.' So, you can say, 'In the *past*, (place in time) he *passed* me by for a promotion.' Or, you could say, 'she *passed* me the pepper.' Or, 'the police car sped *past* me.' Or, 'the police car *passed* me on its way to the accident.'

🐃 : Remember, the 't' in *past* is for 'time.'

Patience/patients

Patience—the ability to accept problems, frustrations, or delays without becoming anxious. Example—he was losing his *patience* when trying to teach his daughter to drive.

Patient, on the other hand, is the adjective, as in, be *patient*. She was a *patient* person. A problem arises (as in the examples above) when we see the singular form of *patients*, which is *patient*.

A *patient*, besides being the adjective for *patient*, also defines 'a person under a doctor's care,' as in, he was a long-time *patient* of the cardiologist. And the plural form, *patients*, means more than one patient, as in, the waiting room was filled with the doctor's *patients*.

🐃 : Remember that *patience* has a 'c' in it, and you have to *control* your *patience*. Control and *patience* both have 'c's.'

Also remember that *patients* (with an 's') always refers to people. So, if you see an 's,' *someone* is seeing a doctor.

Peace/piece

Peace is what you experience when you're not at war. The *Pax Romana* was one of the longest durations of *peace* the world has known.

Piece is a part of something larger, as in, please cut me a *piece* of pie, or I'll have a *piece of cake, please*.

The issues of confusion seem to arise more with associated sayings than the words. Example—I'll give him a *peace* of my mind. ✗
It should be I'll give him a *piece* of my mind. ✓
To give someone a 'piece of your mind' is to let someone 'share' your thoughts. Imagine you are reaching in and 'slicing' off a piece of your mind.

The real confusion arises due to the other saying, 'Peace of mind,' as in, all she wanted was a little *peace of mind*. In this case, the person wished for her mind to be at rest, in other words, *not to war* with itself.

🐃 : To remember this, think of actually *slicing* a *piece* of your mind and giving it to someone. In that case, it's going to represent 'a piece of mind.' If you *want* peace of mind (something good/desirable), then you're talking about *peace*.

🐃 : Remember, *peace of mind* is something you want. A *piece of your mind* is something you give.

Peak/peek/pique

Peeked/Peaked/Piqued —If you're going to use one of these words— especially on a résumé— make certain you use the right one.

Peeked, is used for things like 'He *peeked* around the corner to get a look at the new neighbor in her bikini.' (I'm not referring to me. No way. Not ever.)

Electricity usage *peaked* during August, typically the hottest month in Texas. (I can vouch for that.) This can also refer to the peak of a mountain.

Dear Gatekeeper: My interest was *piqued* by reading an article on the company's new product. (Ah! There's the definition we were searching for.)

🐘 : Remember that *peeked* is similar to looked and they both have repeated vowels, and that *peaked* is like a mountain peak.

Pedal/peddle/petal

A *pedal* is something you control with your foot, as in, the *pedal* of a bike, or the gas/brake *pedals* on your vehicle.

To *peddle* is to sell. In the old times, it meant door-to-door, or, in even older times as *peddlers* in wagons. Now it has come to mean something different, as in, he *peddled* his drugs too close to the school.

A *petal* is one of the colorful parts of a flower.

🐘 : Remember that a *pedal* is something you use, *peddle* is something you might do, and a *petal* is something you might want.

Peer/pier

A *peer* is, in one sense, an equal, as in, a jury of his peers. It also means to look or stare in order to obtain a clearer sight.

A *pier* is a shipping dock. It is usually built on 'legs' and begins on land, stretching into the water so that ships can moor there and load or unload cargo.

🐃 : Remember that to *peer* is to *see* or *look*, and all of them have repeated vowels at the beginning.

People/persons

A *person* refers to one. *People* to more than one, as in, there were a lot of *people* at the beach. *Persons* used to be the plural of *person*, but common usage has substituted *people*.

Missing *persons* and *persons* of interest are a few examples where you still see *persons* used frequently. It seems to be used more in 'law enforcement' situations than anything. If you want to be safe, if it's more than one *person* you're referring to, use *people*.

Perpetrator/suspect

As any loyal fan of crime shows can tell you, a *perpetrator* is the person who *did* the crime, and a *suspect* is a person *suspected* of being a *perpetrator*.

Example—the police arrested a *suspect* for the robbery, but he was not the *perpetrator*.

🐃 : Remember that a *suspect* is only *suspected* of a crime, he/she didn't necessarily commit the crime.

Persecute/prosecute

Prosecute means to start legal proceedings against, as in, the assistant district attorney decided to *prosecute* him for murder.

Persecute means to harass or torment, especially if related to religion, race, or sexual orientation. Example—the pilgrims were *persecuted* for their religious beliefs.

🐾 : Remember that *prosecution* begins with *pro* and it is usually (or should be) good.

Peruse

Peruse means to examine carefully, or at length, but it is often used in the opposite sense, as in, I *perused* the résumé when they really mean, I *scanned* the résumé. Some dictionaries even offer alternate definitions of *peruse* now—to read casually, which is the opposite of thoroughly. Common usage is such that you *could* use it either way, but for the sake of consistency and clarification, I'd stick with one or the other, and preferably, the right one.

Per se/per say (Per se is Latin meaning 'as such' *per say* is not a saying.)

Per se is from Latin, and means *by itself,* or *in itself,* as in, Stealing a loaf of bread to feed your child, does not, per se, mean you are a thief. Why would you say this instead of just 'by itself?' I don't know, but if you are *wont* to use the saying, do it properly.

Per say is simply a common misspelling of *per se*, so it is *not, per se*, such a grievous error.

🐟 : Remember the 'y' in *per say*, and think *why* would I use the one with 'y?'

Plethora

Plethora does *not* mean a lot. It means *too many, an overabundance*. An example might be—the pond had a *plethora* of fish, meaning there were too many fish to live comfortably (or even too many to live). But you probably wouldn't say Baskin Robbins has a *plethora* of ice cream flavors (unless it was so many you couldn't make up your mind).

Poisonous/venomous

If you're ever on a quiz show and the question is 'How many *poisonous* snakes are native to North America?' — the answer is *none*. A snake is not *poisonous*, it's *venomous*.

Certain tree frogs are *poisonous*. Some plants are *poisonous*. But anything that needs to bite or sting you to make you sick is considered *venomous*, therefore all *poisonous* snakes are actually *venomous* snakes. (There is one exception that I know of. The Asian Tiger Snake is considered to be *venomous and poisonous due to a diet of poisonous toads*.)

🐟 : It's simple to remember. Things that are *poisonous* need to be touched or drank, while *venom* needs to be injected.

Pore/pour

Pore is a small opening, as in, the *pores* of your skin, and, in the verb form, as in, *to pore over*, means to read/study something intently, as in, he *pored* over the law book. Note that *pore*, when used as a verb, is almost always coupled with 'over or through.'

Pour, on the other hand, is to flow, as in, he *poured* the customer a beer, or it's going to *pour* (rain). It doesn't have to be liquid, either. Think of 'pour the sand out of the bucket.'

🐎 : Remember that *pour* and *out* both have the letters 'o and u' in them, and you often use 'out' with pour, (as in, pour out the sand) but you never use *out* with *pore*.

Precede/proceed

Precede means to take place before something else, as in, the *discovery* of America *preceded* the Revolutionary War.

Proceed is a verb meaning to move forward, continue what you were doing, keep at it, etc., as in, *proceed* to the counter, please.

🐎 : It's easy to remember the difference, as *precede* begins with *pre*, which means before.

Premise/premises

The *premise* is a proposition upon which an argument is based, as in, the *premise* of her argument was...

Premises is a site, as in, the police searched the *premises*.

🐘 : Think of the 's' at the end of *premises* as meaning 'site.'

Presence/presents

Presence is an opposite of absence, in other words, *presence* means the state of being present, in existence. It can also mean a person's state of mind, as in, she had the *presence* of mind to remain calm.

Present can be a noun, meaning a gift, as in, he gave her a bracelet as a *present*. It can also be a response to 'roll call,' as in, when a teacher calls your name and you respond, 'present,' meaning you are 'there,' you are in attendance.

Present might also be a verb meaning *to introduce formally*, as in, he was *presented* to the ambassador.

Presents is the plural of present, as in, he received many *presents* at Christmas.

Preventive/preventative

There has been a heated argument over the usage of these two words, and yet, common usage shows *preventative* gaining ground.

Some people subscribe to the theory that *preventive* is an adjective and *preventative* is a noun, but there is no basis for this argument. As far as I'm concerned, use *preventive* and save a few letters.

Phase/faze

Faze is a verb meaning to disturb or bother, as in, he wasn't *fazed* by her flirting.

A *phase* is a stage someone/something goes through, as in, she was influenced by Madonna, and went through a *phase* of dressing skimpily. Or, the moon is in the first *phase*.

🐃 : Remember that the father wasn't *fazed* by his daughter's *phase*.

Principal/principle

Principle can only be used as a noun, as in, a person of moral *principle*. A *principle* is *not* a person, so it is *never* a school *principle*. It is a school *principal*.

Principal can be a noun or an adjective, so you might pay the *principal* on a loan, go see the *principal,* or be the *principal* (main) person in a movie or stage production.

🐃 : Remember that a 'pal' is a person, and *principal* ends with 'pal,' so the school superintendent is the *principal*.

Prostate/prostrate

To *prostrate* means to lie face down on the ground, usually in supplication, like they did for the old kings and queens. There is no *prostrate* gland, or cancer of the *prostrate*.

When referring to the gland that is near the bladder, it is *prostate* — no 'r' after the 't.'

So if you hear that someone has a *prostate* problem, it doesn't mean that they have a problem lying (not laying) in front of their monarch.

🐎 : Remember that *prostrate* contains an extra 'r' and the word recline also contains an 'r.' Both mean to put yourself in a certain position, either reclining or lying down, as opposed to *prostate*, which is a gland.

Raise/raze

Raise and *raze* can almost be opposites. To *raise* something up means to *lift it*. To give someone a *raise* means to increase their pay. But to *raze* something is to tear it down, as in, the Romans *razed* the city of Carthage after the Third Punic War.

🐎 : Remember that *raise* is contained in the word *praise*, and that they are both something good.

Rapped/rapt/wrapped

This is another triple homophone. All sound the same, but have different meanings.

Rapt means to be engrossed in thought, or *focused on another place*. I believe the word 'rapture' comes to us from the same root words.

Rapped is the past tense of 'rap,' meaning to tap or knock on the door, as in the line from Edgar Allen Poe's, 'The Raven' — ...*rapping* at my chamber door.

Wrapped is the past tense of *wrap*, and means to cover something on all sides, as in, she *wrapped* all of the birthday presents in *princess paper.* Or, he was cold, so he *wrapped* himself in a blanket.

🐃 : Remember that *rapt* is similar to *rapture,* and *rapped* is like a *rap star,* and *wrapped* is like *wrap* a Christmas present.

Redundant

Something *redundant* is not needed, or in excess. Example—some computers have *redundant* parts that are only there to function in case their duplicate parts don't. Something that is not needed, as in, the welder's job became *redundant* with the purchase of the new robot.

A *redundant* phrase means one of the words is unnecessary, usually because it is implied in the other word. An example might be 'advance notice,' as in, the landlord gave me advance notice that the exterminator would be there. Isn't that the same as, 'the landlord gave me notice that the exterminator would be there?'

As you can see in the previous sentence, 'advance' wasn't needed; it was *redundant.*

Reign/rain/rein

This is another triple homophone, and it is widely confused. First let's look at the differences, then we'll see how to distinguish them.

To *reign* is to rule, as in, the king was benevolent and his *reign* was good. He *reigned* for 54 years. As you can see in the preceding sentences, *reign* can be a noun or a verb.

Rain is a liquid that falls from the sky, as in, it's going to *rain* like hell. It has come to mean other things, as in, the 1980s song by the Weathergirls, 'It's *Raining* Men,' meaning there was an abundance of men.

Reins are the leather straps that you might use to control a horse. *Rein* is also the word used in the sayings 'Give it free rein' or 'Rein it in.'

🐃 : So, how to tell the difference? Try thinking of the 'g' in *reign* standing for *gold*, and a king or queen should have *gold*.

🐃 : Or, think of *rain is a pain.*

Regard/regards

In regard to…
In regards to… or *as regards*
Regards or 'with regards'…
Regarding

You might see any combination of these terms, especially in business writing. They are used when referring to something, as in, *in regards to the project…* Or to close out a letter, as in, With *regards*, or, *regarding the meeting…*

The definitions are a bit confusing as well. There are so many, you might end up scratching your head. *To hold in high esteem, to look at, to consider, to show respect for, and more.*

Most style guides consider 'in regards to' or 'with regards to' as nonstandard, preferring 'in regard to' or 'with regard to' or even 'regarding.'

🐂 : I have a standard rule that I try to follow. If I am going to use 'to,' I never use the plural—regards—and always use the singular—regard. So, I would write, *in regard to or with regard to,* not *in regards to* or *with regards to.* Of course, I usually abandon both choices and opt for the simpler, *regarding*, instead.

If you're looking for a way to refer to something/someone, try using *regarding.* If you want to close a letter, there are plenty of other ways to do that, casual and formal. Try *sincerely, warmly, thanks, thank you, etc.*

🐂 : If you decide to stick with *regard* (singular), remember that you don't use *anyways, afterwards, onwards, or towards,* and you *don't* use *regards.*

Regime/regimen/regiment

A *regime*, by definition, is a system of rule or a government. An example would be, *Hitler's regime* did not tolerate religious freedom.

Regimen is a guide for living, as in, she had a strict diet and exercise *regimen.* People often use *regime* to mean *regimen*, and it has become accepted. What is *not* accepted is using either one in place of *regiment,* or vice versa.

A *regiment* is a military unit, so unless you are literally walking behind a cohort of Roman soldiers, so to speak, you would *not* say, 'I follow a strict *regiment.*'

🐗 : The 't' in *regiment* is for *troop*.

Reiterate

Reiterate means to repeat, again and again, excessively.

The problem comes in because *iterate* also means to repeat, so *reiterate* would mean to 're-repeat.'

I'm sure I'll catch all hell for this, as this is one of those words that has gained widespread use and recognition, but if I were you, I'd steer clear of this, and especially the saying *let me reiterate*. Do you need permission? Why not just say it?

Some people say that *iterate* is for an *action* that's repeated, and *reiterate* is for words, but I don't buy it. As far as I'm concerned, say it once. If they don't understand it, shame on them. If they didn't hear you, speak louder next time.

Resume/resumé/résumé

Resume means to start again, as in, *resume the position*.

Résumé is a noun. It is a document that is a summary of your work history.

As a verb, you have no problem. *Resume* (pronounced re-zoom) cannot be confused with *résumé*. But the spelling can still be an issue. *Résumé* is derived from French (meaning to sum up), and diacritical marks are used to distinguish the spelling. The problems arise because most people, myself included, are too lazy to type *résumé* the way it should be. They end up typing it as *resume*. I was chided for this in my book—*No Mistakes Resumes*. That chiding did the intended job, though, as I immediately made a typing 'shortcut' for *résumé* so I wouldn't have much trouble in the future. (If you want to see more writing shortcuts, see the book I wrote about it.)

In most cases you don't have to worry. I think the majority will be able to decide, based on context, which one you mean, but if you want to be safe, take the time to write *résumé* instead of *resume*.

Retch/wretch

To *retch* means to vomit, as in, the sight of the mutilated body was so grotesque even the veteran detective wanted to *retch*.

A *wretch* is a person of disgust, an undesirable character. We usually think of a wretch as being old, but that's not a necessity.

🐗 : The stench of the *wretch* almost made him *retch*.

Review/revue

A *review* (when used as a noun) can be a critique of a work of art, as in the critic *reviewed* (verb) the play, or the movie, or the NY Times *review* (noun) of his book was not flattering.

As a verb, *review* means to reconsider, look over again, or critique something.

A *revue* is (usually) musical entertainment that constitutes a parody of current events or personalities, as in, the *revue* parodied President Obama.

🐃 : Remember that *review* contains the word 'view' and one of the definitions of *review* is to 'look' over or 'look at again.'

Riffle/rifle

These are commonly confused words, in spelling *and* meaning. As a verb, *riffle* means to shuffle cards, or to flip through a book, or to skim a stack of papers. It can also be something that causes *ripples* or waves in the water.

To *rifle* something means to search for something in a hurry, as in, the burglar *rifled* through the file cabinet. It can also be used for the more common usage meaning weapon, as in, the *rifle* was actually a musket.

🐃 : The origin of the word *rifle* was *to plunder* and it keeps that connotation when used as a verb, as in, he *rifled* through the cabinet looking for the files he wanted.

Riffle is more like *shuffle*, and they both have two 'f's.'

Right/rite/write/wright

This is one of the only quadraphones (I don't know if that's even a word.) that I know of. On top of being possibly unique for that reason, it is confusing to a lot of people. Let's try to work out the problems.

Right is the opposite of left. It also means correct. In addition, it can mean permission, as in, she has the *right* to do that.

Rite is a ceremonial act, as in, a wedding *rite*.

Write is to place words on paper, or a tablet, anything—even a computer screen. *Write* is the present tense of *to write*.

Wright is an old word brought to us from the English. It meant a worker, so shipwright is a derivative, as is a word you might be more familiar with—*playwright*.

➤ : Remember that you have the *right* to *write* anything. Who knows, you might even become a *playwright*.

Role/roll

Role is the only one of the two that refers to a person, as in, the actress accepted the *role*, or she was a great *role* model. *Roll* refers to movement of some sort, as in, he rolled the ball, or the plains of Kansas seemed to *roll* on forever, or he responded to the *roll* call, or 'rock 'n' *roll* or tears rolled down her cheeks, or the river rolled through the valley or the thunder rolled. As you can see, *roll* usually refers to movement of some sort. There are, however, exceptions: *roll* call, a scrolled parchment, etc.

➤ : My suggestion is to think of the differences as mentioned—*role* refers to a person, and *roll* to movement. In the event you experience the other kinds of *roll* (*roll* call or a scroll of parchment), you'll have to remember them.

Rung/wrung

A (usually round) piece of material that forms the steps of a ladder, as in, the ladder had sixteen *rungs*. The piece between the legs of a chair that strengthen it, as in, he rested his feet on the *rung* of the chair. The metaphorical steps of a company ladder, as in, the new CEO used her knowledge of company politics to climb to the top *rung*.

As a verb, *rung* is the past perfect tense of the verb to ring. An example is 'If you don't arrive before 1:00, I will have *rung* the bell for the waiter,' or, 'the child knew she was late for church as the bells had already *rung*.'

Wrung is the past tense of wring, as in, she *wrung* her mop dry, or, she *wrung* her hands dry worrying about her son.

Wrung is a verb meaning to squeeze, or twist. *Rung* is the past tense of ring, or the 'steps' of a ladder, etc.

🐘 : Remember that you can't climb a *wrung* and the telephone can't be *wrung*.

Set/sit

Set and *sit* are often confused, yet it's easy to distinguish the difference. *Set* is a *transitive verb*. I know this is getting technical, but I listed it so you might understand that *set* requires an object, and *sit* does not. So, you need to *set* 'something,' whereas, you can *sit* by yourself. So, you can order your dog to *sit*, but you need somewhere to *set* your coffee cup. (It's similar to *lie, lay, and laid* and can be used to substitute for those words.)

🐃 : Remember, an animate object *sits*. But an inanimate object is *set*.

Sear/seer/sere

Another triple homophone.
A *seer* is a person who says they possess the ability to 'see' the future, as in, the *seer* swore he could see a war coming.

To *sear* is to burn, as in, he *seared* his arm while grilling the steaks.

Sere is an adjective meaning dried up or withered, as in, the desert consisted of *sere* vegetation.

🐃 : Remember that a *seer* says he can 'see' the future.

Shear/sheer

To cut a sheep's hair/wool, as in, he *sheared* the sheep.

The farmer missed with the hammer and *sheared* the bolt.

It was a *sheer* cliff—very steep.

The woman wore a *sheer* blouse, but none of the men complained.

What he said was *sheer* nonsense.

🐗 : Remember that *sheer* has two 'e's' and *steep* has two 'e's.' And *shear* contains the word *ear* and you have to be careful when you *shear* a sheep's *ear*.

Shudder/shutter

A *shutter* is a louvered cover for windows. In the past, I think all, or most, houses had *shutters* on the windows.

To *shudder* is to shake or convulse because you are cold, or perhaps afraid. It was so cold his teeth were chattering and he was *shuddering*.

🐗 : If it's cold, your body might *shudder,* but you must close the *shutters*.

Silicon/silicone

Silicon is an element that is commonly found almost anywhere on earth. It is a great conductor of electricity and is used as the basis for microchips. Silicon Valley (the area south of San Francisco was named that because so many companies used *silicon* in the manufacture of the chips.)

Silicone is a synthetic polymer that is used in many products, including *silicone* breast implants.

🐗 : Remember that *silicone* has an 'e' and it is made from a *synthetic*/fake substance, and both synthetic and fake also have an 'e.'

Slay/sleigh

To *slay* is to kill someone or something, as in, the hero of a video game might have to *slay* a dragon and rescue a princess.

A *sleigh* is something usually used to ride on snow. It is typically made of wood and has metal rails. Some places (especially romantic getaways) offer horse-drawn *sleigh* rides.

🐎 : Remember that *slay* is spelled similarly to *pray*. The princess had to *pray* that the knight would come to *slay* the dragon.

Sleight/slight

Sleight is derived from an old word meaning cunning or sly. You seldom see it used now, except in the saying, *sleight of hand*, referring to a magician's skill in manipulating something with his hands.

Slight (without the 'e') is a word meaning small or insignificant, as in he is *slightly* taller than his wife, or, the knife slipped and he received a *slight* cut. Or, the lack of an invitation was a *slight* that she couldn't tolerate.

🐎 : Remember that *slight* has the word *light* in it, and a *slight* and *light cut* are similar.

Sneaked/snuck

These words both mean the same thing—the past tense of the verb to sneak. *Sneaked* is the preferred usage, though *snuck* is gaining ground. This is an *irregular* verb, and as such, is one of those that has to be committed to memory, as it follows no rule.

So to speak — meaning

So to speak is used to indicate that the preceding sentence/statement is not necessarily *literally* true, but perhaps in a metaphorical way, as in, the dog was his baby, *so to speak*. It means that the dog wasn't really his baby, but he treated it as if it were.

Some time/sometime

This is another of those words, like some one/someone or any where/anywhere, etc.

Sometime means at an indeterminate point in time, as in, he is going to San Francisco *sometime* next month.

It had been *some time* since he'd been to the book store.

🐗 : Remember, if you can use 'a long time' or 'a short time' in place of the word, you're looking for *some time*. Example—It had been *a long time (some time)* sine he'd been to the book store.

But you couldn't say 'he is going to San Francisco *a long time* next month.' (You might say *for* a long time, but not a long time)

Stair/stare

A *stair* or *stairs* (usually referred to in the plural form) is a platform or set of steps that exists between two floors of a home or building. He climbed the *stairs* to reach the second floor.

To *stare* at something/someone is to look at them (focus on them) without blinking, usually for an extended period of time. I know you've heard *somebody's* mother say, 'it's not nice to *stare.*'

🐘 : Remember that *stair* contains the word *air*, and a long set of *stairs* goes into the *air*. Also, *glare* and *stare* are spelled similarly.

Stationary/stationery

Stationary is an adjective meaning in a set place, not moving, as in, he was driving wildly and hit the *stationary* car.

Stationery is a noun which refers to office supplies or writing materials, as in, I need some pens and paper clips so I'm going to the *stationery* store.

🐘 : This is one of those words that you might have to commit to memory. If you think of a tip to remember the difference, let me know.

Steal/steel

Steal is a verb which means 'to steal' or take from someone without paying. It can also be used as a noun (slang), meaning a bargain, as in, the price on that TV is a *steal.*

Steel is a hard metal made from iron and carbon, as in, Superman is known as the 'man of steel.'

🐘 : Remember to think of Superman as the 'man of steel' and you'll know which spelling to use. After all, Superman wouldn't *steal.*

🐃 : Also, some *wheels* are made of *steel* and they are spelled in a similar fashion.

Straight/strait

A *strait* (without the 'gh') is a narrow body of water connecting two larger bodies, as in, the Bering Strait separates Alaska from the Soviet Union, and connects the Pacific Ocean with the Arctic Ocean.

Strait can also mean bound tightly, as in 'straitjacket' or 'straitlaced.' (Not straightjacket—although it is recognized—or straight-laced) *Straight-laced has now come to be, not only, a variant spelling, but a variant meaning.*

S*traight-laced* means a person rigid in their views, while *strait-laced* refers to the more traditional meaning of narrowly bound, as in, the slim girl's movement was restricted by the *strait-laced* corset.

In the plural sense, *straits* means in a difficult situation, as in, having lost everything in the stock market, he is now in dire *straits*.

A *straight* is a hand in poker, not as good as a flush, but better than three-of-a-kind.

It can also mean without bending, no angle, as in, can you draw a *straight* line?

Or, *the shortest distance between two points is a straight line.*

Honest and upright, as in, he'll make you a *straight* deal. A sober person, free from drugs or alcohol, as in, he's straight now. Cops often ask you to walk a *straight* line as a means of testing for alcohol.

Tack/tact

Tact is the ability to deal with, or sensitivity to, social or political situations, as in, the ambassador was hired due to his *tact*.

Tack is a less-often used, but quite often misused, word that means opting for a different course or a different approach, as in, to change *tack* (not change tact).

Tack can also mean to 'add to' as in the state 'tacked' on a surcharge of $1.50 per pack on cigarettes.

Furthermore, it can mean a small nail, as in, he pricked his finger with the thumbtack, or, he used a *tack* to hang the calendar on the wall.

Quote: Isaac Newton said *tact* is the art of making a point without making an enemy.

Taught/taut

The new Spanish teacher *taught* us the language of the streets.

Taught is the past tense of teach, as in, he *taught* us Latin.

Taut is to pull tightly, as in, the continual use of steroids had pulled the skin *tautly* across his bones.

🐀 : Remember, he *taught* me how to catch a snake, and he *caught* the snake. (caught—the past tense of catch is spelled like *taught*.)

Tenet/tenant

A *tenet* is a belief, an opinion, or a principle (usually held to be true).

A *tenant* is a person who rents an apartment, a house, land, an office—anything for a limited time.

🐗 : Remember that *tenant* has the letter 'n' as does 'apartment.'

Than/then

Than and *then* are two of the most confused words ever, and yet there is a simple rule to follow to distinguish the difference.

Than is used for comparison.
Then is associated with *time*.

It's probably best to *show* you with examples.

I would rather play golf *than* swim.
Let's play golf, *then* go swimming.

As you can see, in the first example, we were *comparing* the options, and in the second example, we were suggesting a *time* or sequence to do things. Let's first do this, *then* we'll do that.

🐗 : Remember that *then* has an 'e' in it, and so does *time*. And *than* has an 'a' in it, and so does *compare*.

🐗 : Since this is such a difficult choice for some people, I'll try to provide another tip. *Than* (which is used as a comparison) has no one-word substitute. In other words, you cannot use another single word that means the same thing. Try it. In the sentence 'I would rather eat a pear than an apple,' try to use another word. You could say 'I would rather eat a pear *as opposed to* an apple,' but *then* it wouldn't be one word.

Then, on the other hand, can have many substitutions (synonyms). Try it. 'Let's watch the movie, *then* we can eat.' Now, substitute 'afterward.' 'Let's watch the movie; afterward, we can eat.'

You can also use *subsequently, after,* and any other synonym that fits. They all don't work in every instance, but in many cases they do.

Their/there/they're/there're

Their is a possessive, as in, 'where is *their* house?' Or 'Which house is *theirs?*'

There is an adverb. In some cases it is the opposite of *here*, as in, 'Do you want to come *here*, or should we go *there?*'

It can also be a noun or a pronoun, as in, '*There* is the golf course I want to play.'

Or, *there* will be hell to pay when she finds out what you did.

They're is a contraction for *they are*, as in, *they're* eating dinner now.

🏇 : Remember, if the word you are looking to use is a possessive, use *their*. If the word is a contraction, and you can use *they are* instead, use *they're*. And in all other circumstances, use *there*.

There's/where's/here's - mistakes

See explanation under 'here's.'

Threw/through/thru?

Threw is the past tense of *throw* and means to propel, or hurl, or cast. It usually means to hurl by hand, as in the young boy *threw* a rock *through* the window. It can also mean to *throw* your voice (as in ventriloquism) or cast a shadow (as in, *throw* a shadow).

Through means to go *through* something, as in, *he went through the traffic signal*. Or, Tarzan swung *through* the trees. It can also mean *to be done with*, as in, *I'm through with that*.

Thru is now listed as a variant spelling of *through*, though it is still not universally accepted. It's okay in informal settings, such as, texting, or emailing a friend, but I wouldn't suggest it for business usage.

Till/until

Till and *until* are interchangeable words. Take a look at these sentences: *We ate till we were stuffed, or we ate until we were stuffed. Or, we watched movies till midnight, or we watched movies until midnight.*

Some people think that *until* is more formal, but *till* is the older word. What *is* wrong is the use of the contraction 'til.

If you want to use *till*, feel safe. If you want to use *until*, feel safe. But if you want to feel safer, use *until*, then no one will question you.

Time (when writing a.m. And p.m. You may use lowercases letters with, or without, periods)

To/too/two

To is a preposition used to express or indicate a motion or direction. The following are examples: *He went to the market. I'm sailing to Italy. Let's go to the mall. Give the ball to her.*

Too means *in addition to, or also.* It also functions as an intensifier meaning excessive, as in, the bathtub was *too* full, causing it to overflow. Or, imagine several teenagers conversing. One says, I'm going to the mall, and another says, I want to go, too (also).

Two is the way to write out the number, 2, as in, I'd like two bags of potato chips.

🐗 : Despite this being one of the most confused homophones, it's fairly easy to remember. *Two* can be substituted with the number— 2. If you can't use 2, then it's one of the other *two*.

🐗 : You have *to and too* left. Think of it this way, *too* has an extra 'o,' so it's the word that means also, or in addition to, as in, I want one, *too*. That leaves only one choice, so if your word isn't one of the first *two*, then the only one left is *to*.

Toe/tow

See 'Toe the Line.'

Toward/towards

Same as *backward/backwards*. In the U.S., use the word without an 's.' If you're in the U.K., use the 's.'

Words that fall into this category are: afterward, backward, forward, inward, onward, outward and toward.

Try to or try and

This is one of the most questioned usage issues in all of grammar. So, which is correct?

It would be easy to say 'try to' was correct, so always use that, but almost all research points to 'try and' as an informal usage that is acceptable. I lean toward 'try to' simply because it sounds better to me, and, there are a few sentences where 'try and' doesn't sound right.

As an example—Bob, try to fix the kitchen sink. Now read it the other way. Bob, try and fix the kitchen sink.

To me, the second example doesn't sound right.

🐃 : If you want an answer, I don't have one, but unless you have a specific reason, I'd suggest using 'try to,' and you'll be safe. Remember the two 't's.'

Very (very very overused)

Another intensifier that is seldom needed. Remove it from the sentence, and see if it truly makes a difference. (Or does it make a difference in your head only?) If it doesn't affect the sentence, take it out. (Or use another word to describe what you're tying to say.)

Vice versa

Vice versa is a saying from old Latin that means *the other way around,* implying the reverse is true. An example sentence might be, *my daughter-in-law loves her children and vice versa.* The 'vice versa' implies that the reverse holds true also—that the children love her.

Want/won't/wont

Want, won't and *wont* are often confused, especially with ESL students. The difference between *he won't go to the movies with his wife,* and *he doesn't want to go to the movies with his wife,* are subtle, but significant.

In the first instance, he refuses to go, and in the second case, he doesn't *want* to go, but he *will.*

Wont is a word that is almost never used. It means *accustomed to* or *usual* (habit). As an example, you might say *he was wont to run every morning.*

➤ : Remember that *want* is one word, meaning a desire or a need, and *won't* is a contraction of two words—will not. You can almost forget about *wont* as it is unlikely you will encounter it.

Ware/wear/where

Ware, or *wares*, represent products that a merchant might sell, as in, the manufacturer sold his *wares* direct to the consumer.

To *wear* is to don a piece of clothing, as in, she *wore* a long skirt. It can also mean to erode, (usually used with *away*) as in, the swift-moving river will soon *wear* away the banks that contain it.

Where is an adverb meaning place, as in, *where* is he, we were expecting him by now?

Weather/whether

There is an almost never-used word (wether) meaning male sheep or ram, but I doubt if you'll ever hear it, so for now we'll concentrate on the difference between *weather* and *whether*.

Weather is the condition of the atmosphere that tells you if it is snowing, raining, sun shining, cloudy, etc. It might also refer to a future condition, as in, the *weather* forecast calls for rain tomorrow.

Whether is used to introduce a *choice*, as in, *whether you go or not, is up to you. Or, it's going to rain whether you like it or not.*

Who vs. That

The general rule is to use who for people and that for inanimate objects (and animals with no name).

Examples: The girl *who* you asked out is my sister. *That rock* is a ten-million-year-old fossil. Molly (name) is the name of the dog *who* bit you. *That* dog is mean. (No name)

Which vs. That

It's not that difficult to know when to use *which* versus when to use *that*; they follow a fairly strict set of rules. For instance, you *would not* say, 'No grocery carts *which* contain more than ten items will be permitted.' Instead, you would say, 'No grocery carts *that* contain more than ten items will be permitted.'

The difference is in what kind of clause it is. Restrictive clauses take 'that' while 'which' is reserved for non-restrictive clauses. A restrictive clause is necessary for the sentence to work, while a non-restrictive clause might provide additional information but, the sentence still works without it.

Examples: 'My van, which has a wheelchair ramp, is black.' As you can see, you didn't *need* to state it had a wheelchair ramp. 'My van is black' would have worked on its own. But suppose you had two vans, and only one had a ramp. In that case, you might say, 'My van, the one *that* has a wheelchair ramp, is black.' In this case, your explanation of the ramp is necessary to select the proper van, especially if both of them were black.

Who/whom

There's an easy way to know which form to use. Substitute *he or him* for *who* or *whom*. If *he* works, then use *who*, but if *him* works, use *whom*. Furthermore, you might need to turn the question into a statement to see if it works. So, in the example of the question—

Who should I talk to? You turn the question around and say, *I should talk to him.*

Since the answer was *him*, the proper way to phrase the sentence would be *whom should I talk to?*

🐘 : Remember to substitute he or him and that *him* ends with the letter 'm,' the same as *whom*.

Who's/whose

This is another often-confused word pair that is easy to rectify. *Who's* is a contraction for *who is* or *who has*.

Examples would be:
Who's got the keys? (Who has the keys?)
Or, *who's going with us?* (Who is going with us?)

Whose is a possessive form of who, as in, *whose car is this?* What you're asking is who owns the car.

🐘 : If you can substitute *who is* or *who has* then the word to use is *who's*. If you can't substitute those words, then the word is *whose*. **There is *never* a case where you could substitute *who is* or *who has* for *whose*.**

Widow/widower

There is a difference between the words—*widow* refers to a wife who has lost her husband, and *widower* refers to a husband who has lost his wife.

I'm not going to wonder how, or why, this distinction came about. I'm more concerned with remembering the difference.

🐦 : The way I remember is by thinking of the black *widow* spider. It's the female whose bite is dangerous, and both the spider and a female who has lost her husband are *widows*.

Your/you're

I was going to add *yore* to this list, but it's seldom used, so I abandoned the idea.

Your is possessive, as in, *is that your car?*

You're is a contraction for you are and can easily be replaced by those words. An example would be, *you're a superstar*. (You are a superstar.)

🐦 : There is a simple way to distinguish the difference. If you can substitute *you are*, then the word you're (you are) looking for is *you're*. If you can substitute *my* and the sentence still makes sense, then the word you're looking for is *your*. Example—*is that my (your) car?* Or, *is that my (your) pencil?*

Redundancies

Everyday speech, television, movies, books, emails, and all other forms of communication are riddled with redundancies.

Most of the redundancies are harmless, of no consequence, but if you want to present yourself in the best light, try learning a few of the more common business redundancies. These appear frequently on resumes, cover letters, job descriptions, and especially in emails.

Getting rid of redundant words tightens up your writing and makes it more clear.

Here is a short list:

- Absolutely necessary
- Advance warning
- Actual facts
- Add an additional
- Added bonus
- Already existing
- And etc.
- At the present time
- Basic fundamentals
- Brief summary
- Cancel out
- Completely eliminated
- Consensus of opinion
- Current trend
- Currently away (or unavailable)
- Different kinds
- During the course of

- Each and every
- Emergency situation
- End result
- Exact same
- Final outcome
- First of all
- Foreign imports
- Former graduate
- Future plans
- Gather together
- Had done previously
- Introduced a new
- Join together
- Joint collaboration
- Later time
- Made out of
- Major breakthrough
- Meet with each other
- Merge together
- Number one leader in
- Never before
- New invention
- None at all
- Past experience
- Past history
- Period of time
- Personal opinion
- Pick and choose
- Please RSVP
- Pouring down rain
- Present time
- Proposed plan
- Reason why
- Regular routine
- Sit down or stand up
- Start off or out
- Sufficient enough
- Twelve noon or midnight
- Ultimate goal
- Undergraduate student
- Warn in advance or advance warning
- Write down

Explanations

Let's take a look at some of these examples and see why they are wrong. I'm guessing that most of them are self-explanatory, but for those of you who would like explanations, here they are.

Absolutely Necessary

If something is necessary, there is no need to use absolutely as a qualifier. It is *absolutely* not necessary; in fact, *absolutely* is seldom needed for anything.

Advance Warning
I would hope that this is one of the *self-explanatory* examples. If not, let's take a look. A warning *is* an advance. You receive a warning *before* it happens, so you don't need to use 'advance' in front of warning. It is 'absolutely not necessary.' So the next time you hear the weatherman say he is providing *advance warning* of an upcoming tornado, or hurricane, or whatever, you can chuckle to yourself.

Added Bonus
A bonus already is an 'added' feature. There is no reason to state it again.

And etc.
Etc. means 'and so forth,' and as such, there is no need to use 'and.' If you use 'and,' what you're really saying is *and and* so forth.

Currently Out of My Office, or Currently Away From My Desk, or Currently Unavailable
Call 30 people, and you're bound to hear this misquote more than a few times. "I'm currently away from my desk right now…" This is a double redundancy. We don't need 'currently' and we don't need 'right now.' "I'm away from my desk" would suffice.

Each and Every
Saying 'I picked *each* tomato in that basket is fine,' as is, 'I picked *every* tomato in that basket.' But saying 'I picked *each and every* tomato in that basket is redundant.'

End Result
The result *is* the end, or the outcome, so 'end' or 'final' is not needed when combined with result or outcome.

Final Outcome

Foreign Imports
I hope you see the humor in this one. An *import* means to bring in from a foreign country, so the word 'foreign' is not necessary.

Gather Together
If a crowd 'gathers,' it is coming together. If a group comes 'together,' they are gathering. So you do not need 'gather together.' Gather the history group, or bring them together, but there is no need to 'gather them together.'

Introduced a New
If you 'introduce' something, you are bringing attention to something 'new.' It is, therefore, already 'new,' so no need to state it.

Join Together
The same reasoning applies here as did in 'gather.' If you 'join' something, you bring it together, so no need to say 'join together.'

Later Time
Later already means a 'later' place in time, so there is no need to say 'time.' It's like the saying 'at the present time.' You can simply say, 'at present' as that already implies 'now,' a faction of time.

As you can see, there is no difference between 'I'll see you later' or 'I'll see you at a later time.' (except you said 3 unnecessary words)

Made out of

Suppose someone asked you, 'what is your suit made from?' and you replied, 'it is made out of wool.' Wouldn't it have been simpler to say it is a woolen suit?

Major Breakthrough

A 'breakthrough' is by definition significant or major, so it is redundant to say 'major breakthrough'

Meet With Each Other

This is one of the simplest redundancies to spot. I can't think of a situation where you need the word 'with' in conjunction with meet. Think of it. I'm meeting (*meeting* is simply a better way of saying 'I'm going to meet') John for lunch, or would you say, 'I'm going to meet *with* John for lunch.'?

Or should you say to your friend, 'let's meet with each other at lunch,' or 'let's meet for lunch.'?

New Invention

A 'new invention' is redundant because 'invention' means *new*, so there is no need to say 'new.' If you want to put a place in time on it, such as the iPad is a 'new' invention, you could say 'the iPad is a 'recent' invention,' or, better yet, be specific. *The iPad was introduced in 2010.*

Past Experience/History

Experience and history, by definition, imply past, so there is no need to state it. You wouldn't say, 'I have past experience as a salesman,' when 'I have experience as a salesman,' would suffice. Of course your experience is in the past; you've already *done* it.

Personal Opinion

An opinion is personal. You don't offer other people's opinion, at least not without qualifying it, so if you are offering an opinion, it is yours — and therefore, personal.

Pouring Down Rain

If it's not pouring *down* rain, which way is it pouring — up, sideways? The *wind* might be blowing it sideways, but it is pouring 'down.'

Regular Routine

A routine is, by definition, regular. You might have a 'routine' of drinking coffee with your breakfast every day at 6:00. That is *not* a regular routine, it is a *routine*.

Sit Down/Stand Up

If someone tells you to sit, where are you going to go — the ceiling, the wall? Or will you 'sit' in a chair or on the sofa? The same applies for 'stand.' *Sit and stand* tell all you need to know about which direction.

Sufficient Enough

Sufficient means enough. The words are synonymous, so they can't be used together. It would be like saying, 'that's a big, large truck.' It just doesn't work.

Ultimate Goal

Ultimate goal is like 'final outcome' or 'end result.' There is no need for 'ultimate.' A *goal* is where you want to get to.

Why Does This Matter?

Because communication matters. When you speak and write you want it to be as good as it can. Don't let something silly like a common redundant word trip you up.

One of the most sought after traits (by all companies) is the ability to communicate clearly and succinctly. Improving your speech and writing skills will help.

Sayings

Shoo-in or Shoe-in

The term, shoo-in, traces its roots to the early days of the 20th century in the sport of horse racing. It was before strict enforcement of rules, and races were often fixed. A shoo-in was used to refer to a horse who many people knew would win, as he was going to be shooed (urged on) into the winner's circle.

In those days, jockeys would often allow a slower horse to win, by holding back the reins on their own, faster, horse. They would do this in exchange for money or a tip of what was going to happen so they could place a large bet on the slower horse who would begin the race at longer odds, and therefore pay more if it won.

It became common terminology to refer to a sure winner as a shoo-in, and since horse racing was a popular sport, it soon spread to the rest of the public. Soon, the term came to be associated with any sure winner. Politicians (especially if the race had been fixed) were often referred to as shoo-ins, as were many other forms of competition.

Sometime along the way, the term shoe-in sneaked into the vocabulary. It even came with its own etymological story—that a shoe salesman might wedge his foot in the door to get his foot in the door so to speak.

In the early days of horse racing, things weren't always on the up and up; in fact, things often weren't right. Races were fixed frequently. You could make a lot of money if you knew which horse to bet on, especially if the odds were right. It soon became a badge of honor or at least a recognition of your contacts, if you got a hot tip on a longshot. And everyone was eager to do just that.

Thumbs Up or Thumbs Down?

I was reading a book the other night, and when I finished I went to write a review for it. I wondered, does this get a "thumbs up" or a "thumbs down?" Since it was a damn good book I gave it a thumbs up. But did I do right?

Whenever I see the symbols on a movie rating or a product, I'm left to wonder—is that a good or bad thing? In the US, the ubiquitous thumbs-up symbol means a good thing. Movies are ranked with the symbols, politicians seem to flash the thumbs up sign at every occasion, and it's become standard fare in sports, by both players and spectators. But…did you know the whole "thumbs up" meaning is wrong?

What Does Thumbs Up Mean?
The gesture stems from the Roman gladiator days, when the editor, (one in charge of the games) had the final say on the fate of a fallen gladiator. The editors were people of high rank, usually a senator, a consul, or even the emperor.

You might not be surprised to learn that politics has been around a long time, and it was firmly established in ancient Rome, so the editors, being savvy politicians, normally sought the favor of the crowd. They would listen to what the public wanted, at least in public.

In ancient Rome, when a gladiator lay (not laid) helpless on the ground, his victor poised above him with sword in hand awaiting a signal, the crowd would vote with their thumbs.

The thumbs up signal was accompanied by a shout of *iugula*, which meant—kill him. (Some scholars believe the signal was more of a turned thumb and not a straight-up thumb gesture. The symbol signified a sword thrust up into the heart.) A thumbs-down signal followed the shouts of *mitte*, or let him go. (Those shouts signified that the victorious gladiator should lay his sword down.)

Origin of Thumbs Down
In either case, the thumbs down gesture meaning 'to kill,' seems to have gained popularity based on a painting "Pollice Verso" done in 1872, by Jean-Léon Gérôme.

In the painting, the crowd has their thumbs down, and the gladiator is looking for a sign from the editor of the games. His opponent's fate awaits that decision. But the painting doesn't clearly show the fate of the fallen gladiator, and people assumed the *thumbs down* meant death.

Popularity
The thumbs up symbol as a good thing didn't gain wide acceptance until after World War II. There are several stories as to how this happened and it might be that both contributed.

One story mentions the China-based *Flying Tigers* who adopted the signal from the Chinese who used it to show appreciation.

Another story attributes it to the pilots on aircraft carriers who used the thumbs-up sign to indicate they were ready to "go up."

In either case, the American GIs picked up on it and spread it throughout Europe. It soon became the one sign to mean "good" or "all is well." Combat pilots around the world still use this gesture today.

Misinterpretations
But just because we accept the thumbs up gesture as good doesn't mean others do. If you're traveling in Sardinia or parts of the Middle East, don't give a thumbs-up to thank someone for their kindness or to signal you liked their food.

According to Roger Axtell's book, *Gestures: The Do's and Taboos of Body Language Around the World,* there are many countries that find that particular gesture quite offensive. Many of the Middle Eastern countries do, as well as parts of West Africa, South America, Iran, and Sardinia. In some of these countries giving the thumbs up signal is equivalent to the ubiquitous use of the middle finger in our own society.

Bottom Line
As to my review of the book, I gave it a thumbs up. But who knows, if not for the painting by Jean-Léon Gérôme, I might have given it a big thumbs down.

Final Note:

If you enjoyed this book (and I don't know how you wouldn't), check out my other books at all online retailers.

You Can Also Sign Up for the Mailing List to Get Free Offers and Special Deals.

http://eepurl.com/kS-IX

Authors live and die on recommendations and reviews, so if you liked the book, please tell someone about it. And if you have a spare moment, I'd love for you to post a review on Amazon or Goodreads, or Apple or B&N.

If you want to keep up with all of the books, go to my website.

http://www.giacomogiammatteo.com/

Other Books Coming Soon

Fiction

A Promise of Vengeance (Fantasy)
My first fantasy, and the first book in a four-book series—the Rules of Vengeance. (Three are already written and the fourth is being outlined.)

Murder Is Invisible ### (going through editing)
Frankie and Nicky are back.

Non-Fiction

- No Mistakes Grammar, Volume II, Misused Words for Business (being proofread)
- No Mistakes Grammar, Volume III, More Misused Words. (being proofread)
- No Mistakes Writing, Writing Shortcuts (being proofread)
- Uneducated—Thirty-Seven People Who Redefined the Definition of Education (being proofread)
- Whiskers and Bear—Volume I of the Life on the Farm Series (sent to editor)

Children's Books

- No Mistakes Grammar for Kids, Volume I—Much and Many (Sent to editor)
- No Mistakes Grammar for Kids, Volume II—Lie and Lay (Sent to editor)
- No Mistakes Grammar for Kids, Volume III—Then and Than (Sent to editor)
- Shinobi Goes to School—Life on the Farm for kids. (working on illustrations)

Get on the mailing list and you'll be sure to be notified of release dates and sales.
Mailing list

Acknowledgments

I wish to once again thank all of the phenomenal help I've received from Tirr and their magnificent team of therapists.

I especially want to thank Laura for her help in physical therapy, and Jenna for her help on speech therapy, and both of them for their undying support and enthusiasm. It has been a tremendous help.

As always, I give more thanks than I can muster to my loving wife, Mikki. You're the best. And you have been the best for forty-seven years.

About the Author

Giacomo (Jim) Giammatteo is a headhunter and has done retained searches in the medical device/diagnostics & biotech/pharma industries for 30 years. He successfully completed more than 500 assignments, and he evaluated, edited, and wrote thousands of résumés. Giacomo has also interviewed and done reference checks on more than 1,000 candidates.

As if that wasn't enough to put him into a small room with padded walls, Giacomo is also a bestselling author of several mystery/suspense novels, including: Murder Takes Time, Murder Has Consequences, and Murder Takes Patience in the Friendship & Honor series; and A Bullet For Carlos, Finding Family, and A Bullet From Dominic in the Blood Flows South series. Other fiction includes Necessary Decisions, Old Wounds, and Promises Kept (coming soon), in the Redemption Series.

His non-fiction work includes No Mistakes Resumes, Book I of No Mistakes Careers, as well as book II—No Mistakes Interviews.

He has also written the No Mistakes Grammar Series, No Mistakes Writing, No Mistakes Publishing, No Mistakes Grammar for Kids, and How to Select a Self-publishing Service, Uneducated, and the Life on the Farm Series for both kids and adults. Giacomo's first fantasy series—the Rules of Vengeance—is coming soon.

In his spare time, Giacomo and his wife run an animal sanctuary with 45 loving "friends."

www.ingramcontent.com/pod-product-compliance
Lightning Source LLC
Chambersburg PA
CBHW071519080526
44588CB00011B/1488